E5 LEADER
"LAUNCH FROM SUCCESS TO SIGNIFICANCE IN LIFE"

PAUL KOOPMAN &
MARK PIERCE

PRINTED IN THE UNITED STATES OF AMERICA

Dedication

I dedicate this book to Mark Pierce who taught me how to be an E5 Leader, and who took countless hours and drank countless cups of coffee with me to help me become the man I am today.

Paul Koopman

Table of Contents

Acknowledgments

Mark: Thank you, God, for all things especially my beautiful wife, Linda, and my children for their support as I grew and changed in living a life of significance. I thank my father, Jack, for his love and encouragement and my father-in-law, Bob Coppolino, for coaching me in my youth about business principles. To my first true mentor, Norm Kizirian, and World Wide Dreambuilders who were strong enough to tell me the truth about myself and what I needed to change I am grateful. I thank Sr. Regina, the Poor Clare Sisters and the clergy at St. Paul's Shrine in Cleveland, Ohio for their daily prayers for my total prosperity- spiritually, emotionally, mentally, physically and financially. I say thank you to my friend, Rick Costello, who helped me gain clarity and understanding about my role in the world of CEOs and my mentor, Mike Garnek, who taught me to peel back the layers of my heart to serve others. Finally, I would like to thank Paul Koopman for being willing to learn, grow and inspiring the book and E5Leader. com and Meredith Koopman for her editing skills and tireless support of Paul and me during the writing process of E5 Leader. I love each of you. In closing, I thank all my corporate friends and contributors to my life. You know who you are and I appreciate each of you.

God bless you all.

Paul: My deepest gratitude goes to my God, who has led me down an amazing path that keeps me on my toes and always exceeds my expectations. Thank you to my amazing wife for always believing in me and helping Mark and me make our words beautiful. To my children, for helping me keep it 'real' and in whom I see the bright future, and to my parents who were always true examples of living lives of value. Thank you to one of our readers, Brian Dean, who believed in what he read. I want to thank Mark who saw something in me that no one else did.

PREFACE

How This Book
Came to Be

This life is a talent entrusted to all of us so that we can transform it and increase it, making it a gift to others. No person is an iceberg drifting on the ocean of history. Each one of us belongs to a great family, in which we have our own place and our own role to play.

~John Paul II

Few souls understand what God would accomplish in them if they were to abandon themselves unreservedly to him and if they were to allow his grace to mold them accordingly.

~Ignatius of Loyola

Mark's Story

My name is Mark Pierce. My good friend and student, Paul Koopman, and I have collaborated on the following materials based on our mentorship together over the last 4 years. I thought it important for me to sketch out a few details about the style of authorship and our mentorship relationship. Paul has written the majority of this book and I have added value as best as I can. He graciously has allowed me the chance to see my life's work in mentoring others reflected in his growth and successes. He and his wife, Meredith, had 2 small children when we met and along came another and another. Paul is a talented, young man with the love and support of an awesome woman. The love and support of a spouse is one of the keys to success in anyone's married life. Paul has an undergraduate degree in History and Theology and a master's degree in the Science of Management; a weird combination when he achieved these goals, but he didn't know he was going to meet me and I would challenge almost everything he learned in school (no offense to the Talented and Well-Schooled that have amassed in our world today!) Education has a profound effect on one's life. You can learn from your own life or that of others. Paul has learned that if you choose the path of learning from others, you must check the fruit on their tree; if they have the results you want, ask them questions and begin learning/mentoring. If they don't have fruit and only have books, be careful: not everything you learn can be duplicated and applied in your own life.

This book contains a flow of concentrated details and relevant stories to illustrate our point of view and teaching. We have done the best we could to weave each of our styles into one. If you read something that seems off-color or perhaps a little simple, it most likely came from me. I have learned everything of great value I know about the business world and success by reading the Book of Life, the Bible, and through mentorship of other men in my life. My story is simple. I have no formal education. I'm a welder by trade, a high school graduate who married my childhood sweetheart and has four awesome children. I began an entrepreneurial venture at age 23 because I got sick and tired of being sick and tired of working for others, making *them* money only to realize that they were not any smarter than I was! I took a leap of faith and began mentoring with other business owners in my sphere of influence. I decided to start my own company, built it to a level of success, sold it, and retired for the first time at age 29. The System tells us we can't retire until age 65, 69, and now 72. I found out retirement was a matter of money accumulated, not age-related. I have since started a few other businesses and have now successfully worked for myself for 27 years.

I arrived at a crossroads in life in 1999. Through mentorship, it was recommended that I teach others how to reach success for themselves by sharing my experience and knowledge. In 2001, my Leadership and Business Coaching business had begun to flourish. I was motivated by Paul in 2011 to co-author a book on the formula I have created, used, and taught to become "blessable" by God and to achieve my dreams and goals.

Please read and write down any questions you have. We are available to reply via the website, www.e5leader.com, and can offer you a quick start. For those of you ready and seeking in depth mentoring and coaching we can be contacted via the website to arrange a time and place to talk live. Enjoy the materials and *God bless you on your journey to success!*

Paul's Story

My father was a brilliant mathematician. Numbers to him came easily; it was a gift that he had. He went to Kent State University to be an actuary. He was planning to work for a large corporation, and most likely make a ton of money doing so. In Dad's senior year of university, he one day happened to sit in on an education class. That class changed his life. After that day, Dad knew that teaching was more aligned with his dreams and goals than being an actuary was.

Dad was an incredible man, a man of great significance as a well-loved high school teacher. As a kid, I just knew him as *Dad*, my buddy, who would throw baseballs in the back yard with me, play pinochle and gin rummy at the coffee table with me, and let me cuddle up to him as we watched the Cleveland Indians on television. As I entered the teenage years, I became too busy for much but my own self, wrapped up in my sports and friends to fully take advantage of his wisdom.

Eleven months after my high school graduation, my Dad had a massive heart attack and died in his sleep. He was only 54 years old. But as my family and I came to recognize in the following days, Dad's legacy was timeless. Our community drew together as we all remembered and mourned the loss of a great man of faith, of family, and of community. The thousands of people that came to show their respect at the funeral home poured out the doors and along the street. The police force had to escort the mourners from the wake to the church, and again, from the church to the cemetery, as the traffic disturbed the normal flow of the city streets. Councilors flooded the schools to support the mourning students. The local news stations made his legacy a part of the evening news.

My Dad was unquestionably a man who made a difference in the lives of others.

To this day, I will meet people who were influenced in some way or other by Dad's *agape* love. He was a man of great character, who recognized that money and position, which he could have easily attained by being a CFO, would not have given him the life of significance that he desired to live. Instead, he followed his aspirations to touch others through his talents, and the decision to be a humble school teacher was the best decision he ever made.

His life and his death had dramatic impacts on me. I realize now that his life was not only a gift for others, but was especially a gift to those he cared most deeply for: his family. He was a man who put God first and himself last. He lived a balanced life, meaning that he put proper emphasis on his spiritual, emotional, mental, physical, and financial facets of life. His optimism and energy was contagious and attractive, and he cared most about his wife and his children and poured out his love abundantly. He was a man of great character.

The impact his death made on my life was something I struggled through for years. After his death, I felt abandoned, that I had lost not just a dad, but my teacher and coach. I was passed those teenage years, becoming a man, and more than ever I was ready to hear his words and learn from his wisdom. I wanted his wisdom that made him significant, his secrets to living a life of fulfillment and happiness. But I had lost him, and I felt entirely lost.

After I completed university and was into my second year of Youth Ministry, married with children, I was living through a particularly difficult time of my life, with much confusion and stress. I had just accepted a wonderful position as Youth Minister at one of the largest churches in the area, and with it came great responsibility.

The new stresses of my job coupled with the anxieties of properly sustaining my growing family put me in a continuous state of feeling inadequate and overwhelmed.

It was at this time that I met Mark. After a church service one evening, he approached me and asked me if I would like to have a piece of pie with him at coffee shop around the corner. I accepted. I began to meet with Mark at French Quarters on a regular basis, and he would pour his wisdom into me, which opened my eyes to a world of possibilities, leadership, balance, hope, and significance.

We talked for hours on end, and for years to come, about building habits that would help me to be a better husband, father, friend, neighbor, countryman, colleague, employee, boss, and most of all, a better person for God who had great plans for me. He taught me to start thinking about my dreams and goals. I marveled at his knowledge, his own history of trials and success, his life of balance, and his goal-oriented nature.

Mark took over where my father had left off. I never thought I would amount to much to speak of, but Mark saw something in me that I didn't see. He became not only my mentor but a friend, a father-figure. He taught me more than just lessons, but the way to a meaningful life. This book is a sliver of Mark's wisdom which he was generous enough to share with me, a collaboration between Teacher and Student who has risen to become Teacher for other students.

PART 1

The Principles
Behind Balance

CHAPTER 1

What is Balance &
Why You Want it

Walk the Line

While driving home from work one day, I came upon the tail end of an interview with a trapeze artist on the radio. My attention was caught when he said something that struck me as odd. He stated that one of the 1st and most important things to learn as a trapeze artist is *how to fall*. I thought to myself, *Hmm, strange. I would think that you'd first want to learn how to balance.* As my mind wandered into the world of trapeze artistry and defying gravity, I eventually arrived at an interesting simile: that life is a lot like walking a tight rope. Imagine yourself high above the ground, and all that separates you from falling is a thin line. You've learned how to fall, just in case your balancing talent doesn't get you to your destination. In life, funny enough, we are all experts at falling: we've learned that part well enough through much experience. But the question is, *have we learned how to **balance**?*

Before we understand *how* to balance we need to know *what* balance is. The 21st century human person is a complex, intricate, multifaceted being. We have spiritual longing, emotional complexities, high mental capacities, physical necessities, and financial realities. And thus, there are five areas in our lives in which we desire—and, as you'll come to understand, require—balance in our lives. Depending on our personal levels of balance or imbalance, these five areas make up who we are and how we act, thus affecting the outcome of life and how we encounter God. The five areas of equilibrium, or E5, are as follows:

1. **Spiritual**
2. **Emotional**
3. **Mental**
4. **Physical**
5. **Financial**

I am sure each one of these areas may resound with you personally – they are familiar to all of us. Take a moment and reflect on how each of these areas that make up our human reality is currently functioning in your life. You could be saying to yourself, *I'm good with God. I am emotionally sound. I read the newspaper. I run twice a week. I know my finances.* Or you may be saying, *Who's God, really? Emotionally, I'm a wreck. I have a no-brainer job that gives me no mental satisfaction. I am 30 pounds overweight. I am in debt up to my ears.*

Chances are, you are somewhere in the middle of these two statements. No matter how you feel about each area of balance, you must take a closer look. Peel away the layers of complexity that make up *you.* I can assure you, becoming balanced in all areas of your life is a lifelong project, albeit attainable and unbelievably satisfying, because becoming balanced *helps you achieve your dreams and goals.* By learning the tools to becoming a perfectly-balanced individual, you will be well on your way to discovering how to maximize your talents and reach your fullest potential in every way.

Doesn't that sound good?

This is where the conversation takes us now: you may not know how to be balanced—that is, fully in control and in harmony—in all these areas of your life. **This book is unique because you will learn the secrets to living a life of total equilibrium and significance. Together, we will uncover the meaning and methods behind balance and success. By the end of this book, you will have discovered the path to becoming who you were meant to be and to fulfillment of your life's dreams.**

What is Balance?

All human nature vigorously resists grace because grace changes us and the change is painful.

~*Flannery O'Connor*

The future is not a gift. It is an achievement.

~*Robert Kennedy*

In everyday life, most of us desire to perform at our greatest potential, to be all that we can be. *Becoming balanced in life is the key to your greatest potential.* Benjamin Franklin said, "A small leak can sink a great ship." Life is far too precious for us to sink into the abyss of own weaknesses and to never achieve the potential that God has given to us, considering we only have one chance at it.

So, what is balance?

Balance is the ability to maintain equilibrium between all facets of your life through self-knowledge, self-mastery, and prioritization, in order to reach your goals.

The five facets of your life, namely *Spiritual, Emotional, Mental, Physical,* and *Financial* each have individual needs. The work to attain balance involves managing, sustaining, and moving forward in your goals, while meeting the individual needs of your Self.

MANAGING YOUR LIFE & GOALS

The proper management of all five facets of your life is a difficult task for any of us. However, proper management of each facet of life gives you a greater ability to attain your dreams. What this means is that *everything is in alignment (equilibrium)*. The Ford

Company created the most efficient, effective mode of manufacturing automobiles: the assembly line. The efficiency and effectiveness, however, would be highly jeopardized if even one of the stations within the assembly line was missing, or not working up to par. The same goes for you: the intricate balance between the five facets of life, or E5, takes proper management and necessitates that everything is in alignment.

Sustaining & Moving Forward with your goals

Every living thing needs water to live and grow. To live a good and healthy life, you must not only maintain it, but sustain it through a healthy lifestyle in every facet of life: spiritual health, emotional health, mental health, physical health, and financial health. In sustaining your overall health, you are feeding your Person and sustaining the forward movement of your goals. *You can properly achieve your highest goals only in achieving total balance.*

Why You Want Balance: Universal Struggles

Pope John Paul II urged his followers many times to "become what you are." It is our duty to understand and encounter the real meaning of our lives. The distractions and temptations that surround us today are pulling us away from becoming the fullness of who we were created to be. Having E5 in all areas of your life gives you focus, energy, and motivation to achieve your life dreams and to become what you really are: an incredible individual with insurmountable capabilities. With proper balance, you can make your life what you want it to be, instead of being pulled along in the daily grind, barely making it by on a spiritual, emotional, mental, physical, and financial level.

1. **Personal Dissatisfaction**

We have all grappled with these questions at one point in our lives:

Who am I? Where am I going? Who am I in relation to this world, in relation to history? What is my purpose?

These questions lead us to an innate anthropological human desire: to be meaningful, to have value, to be *great*. There is a place deep down in each one of us that desires to be great – to be someone that truly makes a difference in this world. Ultimately, our desires were put into us by the One who created us. If God placed those desires in our hearts, then He would want us to fulfill those desires. In other words, you aspire to be who God created you to be, *and He aspires you to be great.*

You need to ask yourself on a regular basis whether you are reaching toward your aspirations. Do you believe that you are taking steps every day to become all that you can be? Most of us can say with certainty that we live with personal dissatisfaction. There are areas in our lives that gnaw at us and break us down little by little, because we believe that we could do better but are not taking steps toward fulfillment and success in these areas of our lives. The worst part is, we don't know what to do about it.

In fact, we often begin to think of ourselves as less than average. The world can grind us down, make us tired and complacent. We tend to step into a little box, curl up in our comfort zone, and evaluate ourselves according to the minimum standards. We live constricted, confined by our own low self-esteem or lack of belief in our abilities. In a nutshell, we allow ourselves to live a life that doesn't amount to much.

Let me ask you about your state of mind right now, at this moment: do you want your life to have purpose? Do you want to reach your highest potential and affect others' lives positively? Do you have desires? Do you believe in these desires? Do you desire to be *good* or *great*?

2. Inability to Meet Goals

Perhaps these questions have caused a feeling of restlessness within you, stemming from the fact that your desires may have, as of yet, been completely unrealized. Perhaps you live in a continuous state of self-directed anger because you do not accomplish any task to your standard. Confusion, anxiety, worry and feelings of being overwhelmed and paralyzed plague those who are consistently unable to meet daily goals. Personal dissatisfaction leads to a sluggish, unmotivated way of life. We choose comfort over change and growth. One of the greatest 20th century fiction writers, Flannery O'Connor, dealt with the realities of a fallen human nature in her short stories. She surmised, "All human nature vigorously resists grace because grace changes us and the change is painful." It is not part of our natural inclinations to look for and embrace change; we are creatures of habit. Rather, we become comfortable in who we are, where we are, and what we do. Comfort becomes our enemy, because we stop challenging ourselves and live complacent lives.

Robert Kennedy said, "The future is not a gift. It is an achievement." If the future is an achievement, we need to change how we live, think, and act in order to attain what we desire. We need to superimpose virtue, positivity, and disciplined structure into the undisciplined structure of our lives. It takes extraordinary effort and sacrifice, but no worthwhile prize is achieved without effort and sacrifice.

3. **Interpersonal Discord**

We are social beings. We need some interaction with people, no matter our temperament. Not many people would choose to live outside of a geographically populated (even remotely populated) area. Most of us belong to a social network, be it a church community or, even at the lowest level of social interaction, an online community.

Consequently, one of the biggest emotional downers comes from discord on the relationship front. Whether it be with your boss, a co-worker, your spouse, a parent, or a friend, the anxiety that results from a breakdown in relationship can drastically throw us off balance. Balance gives you the tools to resolve relational disturbances through your actions and reactions, one of the many benefits of living a full life of balance.

CHAPTER 2
Balance in Detail

Let us get down to the details of E5. Our lives are in such a state of constant motion, from one activity to another, one responsibility to another that we often forget to stop and breathe, or to consider that there ought to be an optimal way to balance our life between every activity. So, how do you interject balance in your everyday life?

What Occupies Our Time: Daily Grind & Distractions

On a regular day, a Regular Joe will divide his time between three main activities: work, relaxation, and personal enrichment. Work can be defined as your job or career, and home management. I will define relaxation time as the time you spend on your own and with others in extracurricular activities such as entertainment and sports. Personal enrichment I define as the time you spend alone or with others, enriching yourself on a spiritual, intellectual, and physical level.

We are all bumping along for the ride, dealing with distractions on a very regular basis throughout our days. In order to be a man or woman of balance with a vision for the future, we must organize our day according to importance and attempt not to be sidetracked by these distractions. We must learn to categorize what is priority for the day, as well as what is priority for the sake of our future. With this organization of mind and spirit, we can bypass many of the daily distractions that frustrate and drain us.

These infuriating bothers that love to divert us from our dreams and goals are a part of life: we cannot eliminate them altogether but we can learn how to control them. This is critical if we are to be serious about achieving our dreams and goals. Before we can control distractions, we must first identify them and define what the distractions are. The following is a list of some significant distractions in life that may prevent us from efficiently achieving our dreams:

- Marriage and family difficulties
- Financial difficulties
- Job promotion
- Major changes in associations
- Health challenges
- Moving houses
- Vacations
- Sports
- Visiting relatives
- Holidays
- Taxes
- Volunteering
- Guilt, sin, and regret

Not all distractions in and of themselves as terrible things. Some are necessary, like filing taxes. The best way to deal with this distraction is to simply *get them done.* Don't procrastinate and allow it to eat away at your mental agility. Other distractions are avoidable, such as vacations or sports. These enjoyable activities can be used as a reward for hard work achieved (first pay, then play!) Some distractions weigh heavily on your spiritual and emotional wellness (and in effect, affect your whole person) such as guilt and sin. The most rewarding way to avoid such distraction is to live a life of virtue and repentance. *This way of life* is *the way to your dreams and goals!*

The most effective and efficient way to live out your everyday life is to keep it organized, with your goal in sight. Goals are met through priorities and habits. Earlier, we mentioned that we must learn to categorize what is priority for the day, as well as what is priority for the sake of our future. I will be going into detail a little later about each of these prioritizations. To explain briefly: daily activities are prioritized through living Vertical Alignment, a declaration of objectives to achieve within your daily decisions. Future priorities are met through discovering and pursuing your 10-10-10, a personal list of dreams and goals.

The Cleansing Process: Eliminating Agents of Paralysis

How do you know that you are prepared to take on this re-ordering of your life? I believe that most of us need to go through a cleansing process in order to be prepared to take on life-changing habits. Let's think of it this way: before I go for my morning run, I need to stretch my body. These stretches prepare my muscles to work at their peak performance level. My wife loves to swim; she knows that if she fails to feed her muscles a good dose of potassium in her breakfast before her 1-mile lap workout, she will be doubled over with cramps halfway through her regimen. This Cleansing Process is our stretches, our vitamins, which prepare us for the journey ahead, so that we can perform at our highest potential with optimal efficiency and effectiveness.

The Cleansing Process is individual to your own situation. It is a soul-searching, honesty-driven time of reflection and courage. Courage is necessary because we are dealing with personal insecurities; it is necessary because, change is difficult, especially change that is demanding. To take the treacherous journey up to the peak of Mount Everest is more challenging than to stand at the bottom looking up. Which experience is more rewarding? Which photograph is more breathtaking: the one looking up, or the one from the tallest peak?

Try to think objectively. Look at your life from a bird's eye view, from the top of Mount Everest. Sometimes we are so used to living the life we live that we have a hard time seeing the difference between our strengths and our weaknesses, determining the difference between what is good and what is not so healthy in our lives. Mark Twain said, "I can teach anybody how to get what they want out of life. The problem is that I can't find anybody who can tell me what they want." Objectivity is achieved most accurately from the help of an honest and good friend or mentor, who can gently lead you to a better understanding of yourself, how you tick, and why you tick the way you tick. This input can be used to formulate the steps to achieve your lifelong dreams.

Step 1: Asking Yourself Questions &
Answering them Honestly

- Is there anything in my past that prohibits me on an emotional level from moving towards my dreams and goals?

- If so, is this my fault or the fault of another? Or is this thing that holds me back no one's fault?

- Do I feel imprisoned by what I consider personality defects?

- What are the negative habits I have that are getting in the way of my forward movement in life?

- Do I have a negative outlook on life? Do I believe that only bad things happen to me?

- Are there any dreams or goals that I desire deeply but I've never attained or tried to attain, and I don't know why I am holding back?

Step 2: Action

- Seek forgiveness for any past wrongdoings through spiritual confession, letters of forgiveness, and words of forgiveness to others.

- Ask for mercy and grace from those you have offended and extend deliberate mercy and grace to those who offend you.

- Build your self-esteem and confidence: write a list of your good qualities to begin focusing on your strengths instead of your shortcomings. Ask a trusted advisor or mentor who knows you to help you write this list.

- Build your positive attitude: Write a list of all the blessings in your life and the good things that have come out of possible bad situations.

Step 3: Counsel—one-time or on-going

- Mentorship can be achieved in person, on the phone, through books, CDs, and other available media.

- Discover your character flaws. Character flaws are thoughts, words, and actions that habitually break either God's laws or man's laws. These flaws are the most common deterrents to achieving your dreams and goals. Discovery of a character flaw can sometimes be a painful experience. It is important to be honest with yourself and to understand that *you only know what you know and don't know what you don't know.* In other words (and as we'll further discuss), the knowledge you possess is only what you've been told or shown, or what you've experienced.

Your actions dictate what you know and understand. A character flaw may be present in you and recognized by everyone but you. Therefore, it is important to seek counsel with a trusted advisor or mentor as a trusted guide in this period of self-discovery. You can then assemble a plan of action (which will be defined in a later chapter) to correct the character flaw(s).

Let's go through all of this together. As you read on, you will see that this process is not scary, but instead something to look forward to, because you will be peeling away the layers of grit and grime to reveal the Real You. It's a journey of discovery. So don't worry—let's discover your fullest potential!

CHAPTER 3

Vertical Alignment: Living with Virtue & Right Judgment

*The more humble a man is and the more subject to God,
the wiser he will be in all things, and the more at peace.*

~Thomas à Kempis

Vertical Alignment is the tool to evaluate, structure, and prioritize your thoughts, relationships, and time, and to properly make key decisions. It is absolutely necessary to follow Vertical Alignment if you want to live a life of balance with E5. Vertical Alignment is the most effective tool to practically apply balance to all five pillars of life. It is a compass which guides you in deciding the level of importance of things by weighing these things up against your goals. This compass, Vertical Alignment, helps you navigate the decisions of everyday life. It is a simple, easy-to-remember method of keeping your priorities straight.

You are a vertically-aligned individual if you keep your priorities in this order:

Married	Single
God	**God**
Spouse	**Parent(s) and/or Children**
Children	**Sibling(s)**
Family Members/Church/ Community	**Family Members/Church/ Community**
Country	**Country**
Job/School/Source of Income	**Job/School/Source of Income**
Self	**Self**

True Vertical Alignment is an act of being in submission to a higher authority. We are all in submission to something in our lives, be it a blessing or a curse. For example, if you are in submission to a bad habit such a smoking, it becomes a type of bondage, making submission a curse. If you have proper vertical alignment and submit to true authority, your submission becomes a blessing to your life. Why is Vertical Alignment so vital to your growth as a person and to your progress in reaching your goals? It is an *order of responsibility* and with responsibility comes duty, which moves you to act appropriately. In a chaotic world, Vertical Alignment provides order.

VERTICALLY-ALIGNED GOALS

With proper Vertical Alignment, your goals and desires can become *blessable*, meaning, God can begin to help you achieve your goals, because your priorities are straight and your goals are pleasing to Him. Managing priorities helps you to evaluate what should be sacrificed in order to achieve a desired goal. For instance, if anything becomes greater to you than God, you are out of alignment and will not feel balance or peace. This may lead to the development of stress and anxiety.

There are many successful men and women who attain their goals at the expense of their marriages or their children. Ultimately, they cannot find fulfillment and happiness in the choices they have made, because their goals were out of alignment, and they sacrificed the greater good for worldly success.

Any time and in any way that Vertical Alignment is broken, it can be fixed, and blessability can be attained. I will show you how to get yourself back on track and how to stay on track, keeping a positive attitude with the knowledge that every moment is a new moment, every day a new day.

VERTICALLY-ALIGNED TIME MANAGEMENT & THOUGHTS

Managing our time ideally is a daily battle for all of us, no matter what our role in life. The reason for this is that the 21st century man and woman has a lot going on: we all have a lot of eggs and a lot of baskets! Keeping up with work, keeping the family relationships strong, keeping in touch with friends and extended family, taking care of cars and bills and pets, keeping up with the kids' education, staying committed to volunteer obligations, staying on top of spiritual and physical wellbeing... these are all things that pull at every one of us on a daily basis. Many of us would admit that we are overextended and cannot apply ourselves 100% to all that we do as a consequence.

The way to ensure that you stay vertically aligned on a daily basis is to revisit this list every morning during your daily reflection time. Go over the day's calendar and schedule in relation to Vertical Alignment. You could ask yourself questions like:

- *Where does God fit in my day? (relational)*

- *Where can I find some quality time with my spouse? (relational)*

- *What area in my life am I putting too much emphasis on? (goal orientation)*

- *In which area can I put more emphasis? (goal orientation)*

- *How am I spending most of my time outside of work? (time management)*

- *Does this volunteer meeting I've set up tonight trump my anniversary in importance? (time management)*

- *Should I answer personal emails tonight before or after I've put the kids to bed? (time management)*

As you analyze your day according to Vertical Alignment, you should be doing a balance check: re-align yourself if you find you are not keeping with the proper order of things. Be honest with yourself. Take two minutes midday to mentally assess how you lived out proper alignment in the morning, and re-align yourself for the rest of the day. Revisit Vertical Alignment at the end of the day by analyzing how your day measured up to proper alignment, and re-assess your game plan in order to be better the following day.

Once this practice becomes habitual, you'll find it a critical part of your day that you cannot live without. It will be a quick, mental check-point which you'll find yourself leaning on for the strength that carries you through each day.

Vertical Alignment presents a guideline to make decisions in life to help you live in balance with E5 and to help you ultimately fulfill your dreams. Vertical Alignment develops within you a culture of thought. You structure your personal time and your thought processes around your Vertical Alignment in order to achieve your dreams and your goals. Of course, aligning your thoughts does not need to always be in the context of time management. For instance, before falling asleep at night, lift up your mind and heart in thanksgiving to God for the blessings of the day, instead of playing over the same scene in your favorite television show for the 100th time that night.

Another tool for consideration to maintain Vertical Alignment is the use of daily affirmations. Two of my personal favorite affirmations that I use, and you can consider adopting as your own when making daily decisions:

- **Does this move me closer or farther away from my dreams and goals?**

- **Will this decision affect my life in a positive way over the next two to five years? If not, is it really necessary for me to invest my time, energy, and resources to this decision?**

When you present these questions to yourself on a regular basis, you become a long-term thinker and develop a culture of thought for the future, not just for the present.

This is precisely why aligning your time is vital to achieving your goals.

VERTICALLY-ALIGNED RELATIONSHIPS

Vertical Alignment puts God first, others second, and you last. It helps you live outside of the egotistical current that pulls today's world around by its neck. It keeps you in harmony with God and in tune to the needs of others, resulting in stronger, deeper, and more satisfying relationships amidst life's daily demands.

Do you love your spouse more than God? Do you spend more time with your kids than you do with your spouse? Do you spend more time with your friends than you do in prayer?

The only things you take with you when you depart from this earth are the relationships that you fostered. Invest your time and heart in the relationships that are the most important. If you truly commit yourself to Vertical Alignment, you will be putting God and his desires for you first and foremost in your life, and the fruits of that relationship will be evident in the rest of your relationships: with your spouse, kids, family members, and all the rest. Go to the source of love and order: God. His love overflows from you into every other godly relationship in your life.

What does this mean on a practical level? Give more quality time, gifts, and acts of service to God than anyone else. When you give to him, he allows you to give more to others.

CHAPTER 4

The 10-10-10: Living with Purpose & Passion

*You are never too old to set another
goal or to dream a new dream.*

~C.S. Lewis

*Success isn't something that just happens – success is learned,
success is practiced and then it is shared.*

~Sparky Anderson

Without self-discipline, success is impossible, period.

~Lou Holtz

For it is in giving that we receive.

~Francis of Assisi

The 10-10-10 is a living and active list that contains your goals and dreams. It is a visible reminder that you read over daily in order to align your daily thoughts and actions to a higher purpose.

The 10-10-10 is not just a helpful way to achieve balance in your life. In fact, you *could* achieve a certain level of balance without a 10-10-10, *but you would not be answering the desires of your heart to become the best person you could possibly be (the real you) if you did not have an active plan in motion,* namely your 10-10-10.

This living and active list helps you achieve many things. First off, *full recognition of your true dreams* comes with the commitment of writing down your own 10-10-10 with focus and purposeful-ness. Furthermore, reading the 10-10-10 out loud daily helps you to *believe in yourself and your goals,* causing your main focus to become the fruition of *achieving them.*

The 10-10-10 is not a purely selfish list of goals, and this is what makes it different from any other "dream list" or "to-do before I die" list that is a more common scenario we often hear about others setting out to accomplish. The importance of your10-10-10 lies in its ability to focus in on your purpose, which is to *be all that you can be through personal growth, selfless offering, and financial security.*

In order to fully take advantage of your personal 10-10-10 you must *read it out loud daily.* Take it very seriously. It should be read in conjunction with scripture, preferably in the morning be-fore you've started your day. You read your list aloud, because *hearing it* strengthens your connection to it. This is the power of the spoken word. Think about this concept for a moment: have you ever read something and realized you don't know what you just read because you weren't paying attention? Your mind was multi-tasking, focusing on one thought while using your eyes to read something unrelated. The mind can't think of two things at one time. When you read your 10-10-10 aloud, you are forcing your mind to engage more fully, using the sense of sound as well as sight to help you absorb what you read more accurately. Leave the quiet reading for the librarians and engage in the power of the spoken word!

Our 10-10-10 list is read with scripture and/or spiritual reading because our goals and dreams should align with the will of God. My 10-10-10 is my Bible's bookmark, which is significant to me on more than one level.

What I have come to love most about living out my 10-10-10 is that is has moved me to live virtuously. I have become malleable to the work of God in my life, allowing him to stretch me like a canvas into the shape and mold he wants. With the 10-10-10, I have moved farther and farther from my comfort zones to become the best possible version of myself. Every goal I focus on makes me rely on my strengths, my desires, and God's supernatural grace more and more. Writing this book has been a goal on my 10-10-10. There were many grueling nights of vigorous concentration in which I felt compelled to give up. I would come up with many excuses to give myself a break and relax. But I knew that, by working this goal, I was being strengthened with the virtues of perseverance and patience. I was being stretched into a better version of myself.

How to Make Your 10-10-10

Here is a mock 10-10-10 for us to analyze together.

SELF. Monetary	SELF. Non-Monetary	OTHERS. Monetary or Non-Monetary
1. I will become 100% debt free	1. I will write a book	1. I will get my wife Lasik eye surgery
2. I will put my family on a weekly budget	2. I will win the club championship	2. I will take my family on vacation
3. I will double my salary by the time I am 45 years old	3. I will pray with my spouse & kids	3. I will go on weekly dates with my spouse
4. I will buy a new car	4. I will be a continuous learner	4. I will visit Florence in the nursing home weekly
5. I will own rental properties	5. I will run the Boston marathon	5. I will teach a local seminar on personal finance
6. I will tithe to the church 10%	6. I will be on the board of my local homeless shelter	6. I will open a library in Nicaragua
7. I will have a savings of 25,000 for each of my children	7. I will learn how to downhill ski	7. I will send a needy family on vacation to Disney World
8. I will retire at a young age with a six-figure income stream	8. I will begin my day at 6:15am every morning for focus time with 10-10-10, scripture, and schedule	8. I will paint my mother-in-law's house
9. I will buy a new home with cash	9. I will stop smoking	9. I will learn all the names of my employees
10. I will give 5% of my income to local needy families	10. I will only watch television 2 evenings a week	10. I will buy Jack a new wheelchair

All of your 10-10-10 goals must be concrete and achievable. *Concrete* implies that these goals have a point of attainment; in other words, you will be able to cross them out one by one in your future. *Achievable* implies that they fit within reality. For example, do not write *I will become an expert ballet dancer in three months,* when it takes about 10,000 hours on average to become an expert at ballet performance. If these goals are unattainable, they will not act as a source of inspiration for your future. Instead, you will feel overwhelmed and frustrated with yourself. I recommend that you sit down with a trustworthy friend or acquaintance who has attained the fruit of success that you desire, and ask him or her to check your list for realism. Be clear that you are not asking for judgment, but only for his or her opinion on the achievability of your goals.

The 10-10-10 is a list of attainable victories. It is a list that helps you gain confidence and build momentum. Sometimes you may lose a battle or two (the Boston Marathon is replaced by a more-achievable local 10k) but this does not mean that you lost the war. This is why a positive and flexible attitude should always be the motivator behind your 10-10-10. (The Boston Marathon could be re-added in two years when it is more realistic.)

The order of achievement of a 10-10-10 remains somewhat mysterious due in part to the nature of *the power of the spoken word.* **What you speak is what you think, what you think is what you believe, and your belief always controls your actions**. There is power in the words and more power when multiplied by faith and the belief that you will achieve the goals and dreams you have set out to accomplish.

Although you take seriously all that you have included in your 10-10-10, it is important to be flexible, as I have mentioned earlier. Your real dreams and goals may not come to you easily; it may take much reflection, prayer, digging down deep to realize your dreams.

I don't want to make this seem difficult; my point is to underline the importance of flexibility and honesty in making your list. (I thought I wanted to learn to play the piano. That was until my family finally got one, and I realized my talents did not lie in music. It would take much time to learn, which would off-balance my Vertical Alignment. My personal desires became larger than the needs of my spouse and family, thus creating a hardship. Although it would be nice to sit down and play *Les Miserables*, it is a personal achievement that will have to wait for a new period of my life, after I have achieved other important goals such as retiring young and debt-free, with a six-figure income stream which would free up plenty of time to devote to the piano. Through discovery and analysis, you learn to be flexible and to reprioritize your order of achievement if needed.

1. **Self**

The list of goals under SELF should be a list that encourages self-discipline, human formation, self-mastery, and personal development, which are all necessary components towards achieving your dreams. These goals should be a mixture of desires and needs. For example, you know that you **need to** *stop smoking* for your own health and for the health and well-being of your family. You've always loved (and been great at) creative writing, and so your goal to *write a book* fulfills a **desire** you've always carried with you.

It is essential, although this section is geared towards your own needs and desires, that you are not selfishly motivated. For example, learning how to *downhill ski* is a desire because it gives you relaxation, exercise, and the enjoyment of nature while spending quality time with your family, who all love to ski. Or, you know that working out 4-5 times a week is part of personal development and can only enhance your quality of life (when properly balanced) and increase your lifespan. Minimizing your time spent watching television helps you balance your time between leisure, responsibilities, quality time with others, and personal growth.

2. **Others**

The OTHERS section can often be the easiest to write down, because it is much easier to be objective about the world and its needs around you than to be subjective about your own personal desires and development. Ralph Waldo Emerson has wisely said, "Make yourself necessary to somebody." This is the purpose of your life: to live with meaning, and to make a difference in the lives of others for the good of humanity. But we have to be prudent about how we give our time, talent, and treasure to others. Giving to others must fit in relation to your Vertical Alignment (which I will talk about in more detail a little later on). You must realize that, if you are married and/or have children, *the needs of your spouse and children are your primary calling in life.* It would be most prudent to *visit Florence at the nursing home* for 30 minutes during a time that does not infringe on family time (like your family's dinner time). This time with Florence should not take away from achieving your dreams and goals, but should complement your life of balance.

Becoming balanced and growing personally gives you the tools to give to others. With the blessings you have been given, you can bless others. By becoming *a continuous learner,* you can increase your knowledge of the people of Nicaragua, for example, in order to meet their needs for a library, which is another one of your 10-10-10 goals.

3. **Monetary Self**

This section might take the most realistic restraint on your part! All of us have played the game before, "What would you do if money was no obstacle?" We'd all dream big dreams of traveling the world, owning a house in the Swiss Alps, giving bundles of money to our favorite charity, owning loge tickets for life to the Super Bowl, etc. It's good to dream big—that's how we achieve our goals!

I grew up in a modest home in a modest neighborhood. We never traveled to exotic getaways, we drove modest (sometimes run-down) cars, and my siblings and I got jobs as soon as we reached high school. My father was a teacher, my mother a receptionist. We were comfortable; not altogether cautious with our money, but rarely extravagant.

I do not know how or why this presupposition became part of my psyche, but I realized later in life, when I embarked upon my journey of personal development, that I somehow viewed prosperity as a reality completely outside of God's realm. After all, *it is easier for a camel to pass through the eye of a needle than for one who is rich to enter the Kingdom of God* (Mt. 19:23). Right?

This Gospel verse needs to be unpacked and examined. Jesus never said that a rich man cannot enter heaven, but that your heart must not serve money and goods.

> *For where your treasure is, there also will your heart be.*
>
> *~Mt. 6:21*

I have been a witness of "millionaire simplicity," which has edified me greatly. A wealthy friend of mine chooses to be detached to his goods, to live in a nice but modest home, to drive a great but used car. He uses his wealth and success to be a blessing to others. He says to love people not things, use things not people. This type of detachment takes incredible discipline and virtue. Because he has worked hard to achieve his financial success through the 10-10-10, along the way he has built the virtue necessary to spiritually handle such success. This is the beauty of the 10-10-10: when you work on bettering yourself in the spirit of Vertical Alignment, God will never give you something that you cannot handle. *If you can't handle the small dealings in life, how will God be willing to give you the big ones?* And so, practicing detachment in all areas of life, regardless of your financial situation, is an important part of your 10-10-10 Monetary Self goals.

And so, it is essential that you believe that prosperity is not a sin, but that, if it is given to you, then it is a gift, and it is good. How we use God's blessings in our lives is the key to our success and happiness. Like all blessings, we must treat the money we have as a way to *serve God, give to others, and become holy.* Answer his promptings, which show themselves as the desires of a virtuous man's heart.

You must also believe that God wants you to be successful. You are created for greatness. God does not create junk! Believe in your desires, your strengths and talents, and believe that you are essential to God's plan for this world. Believe that you *do* make a difference in this world.

Financial success is a part of personal success. Financial success is a natural bi-product of living of the 10-10-10 and Vertical Alignment. Financial success does not only apply to a certain monetary wealth gain. This is not a mathematical equation. You can be financially successful as an outstanding school teacher who has a good retirement, handles his finances responsibly, and who has secured a happy home and future for his family.

The MONETARY SELF list in your 10-10-10 must answer the needs of yourself, your family, and must apply to your dreams. For example, becoming *100% debt free* ensures a stress-free lifestyle for yourself and your family. Giving *5% of your income to local needy families* answers to your call to be a Good Samaritan. Make sure that all of your goals sum up to be financially realistic; they do not add up to a list that takes you well beyond your means. Additionally, be careful to make each goal *individual*, meaning that they are not duplicates just written in another form.

10-10-10 RELATING TO VERTICAL ALIGNMENT

In working to achieve your 10-10-10 dreams, you must be mindful of their relation to your Vertical Alignment. And so, on a daily basis, assess which steps you will be taking to achieve your 10-10-10 goals, and in what order or importance based on Vertical Alignment. By doing so, you will ensure that your life's balance is maintained; in other words, you will not allow yourself to obsess over goals (an imbalance of your mental and/or emotional pillar), and you will have peace knowing that you are staying within God's will for you in accomplishing your goals.

True dreams of the heart (in other words, aligning your dreams with God's Will/dreams for you) will be a blessing to yourself and to others. If you are doubting the alignment of your dream to God's hopes for you, ask a trusted advisor if the dream is in Vertical Alignment. Not only should your dreams stay within Vertical Alignment, but they should be subject to the authority of God's laws and man's laws (moral, ethical, legal).

What profit would there be for one to
gain the whole world and forfeit his life?

~Mt. 16:26

GETTING STARTED

Once you have established your 10-10-10, it is time to take action. Write your 10-10-10 down in whatever way is most comfortable to you: let the style be your own. Whether on an 8x10 paper folded in two, or on an index card, typed or hand written, make it mentally and visually friendly, since you will be reading it over daily. Have it be attainable, easy to keep with you.

As I have mentioned before, my 10-10-10 is in my Bible, marking my page. I have it hand written on an index card. I began reading it every morning with a chapter of Scripture. After the 21-day mark, knowing that this was a habit I would keep for life, I began to have a good feel for the dreams I had scribbled down on this all-important index card. I knew that God was right smack in the middle of my goals.

After reading scripture and my 10-10-10 (in that order), I look over the list of Vertical Alignment and say a small prayer over it, which goes something like this:

God, help me to put you above all else.

Help me to love and protect my spouse.

Help me to teach and cherish my children.

Help me to be a good son, brother, nephew, uncle, and grandson.

Help me to be kind and loving to others.

Help me to be a good citizen of my great country.

Help me to be good co-worker and employee.

Most of all, help me to be the best person I can possibly be, the way you intended me to be.

Next, look over your day's calendar. See where your 10-10-10 fits into your day. Are you doing anything today that will lead you closer to your dreams and your goals? Do you have any plans today that are going to hinder your movement towards your dreams and your goals?

Look at your day's schedule according to Vertical Alignment. When are you going to give time to God? How are you going to show your spouse you love him or her? What is your attitude going to be today towards your not-so-nice co-worker?

Take this time to mentally prepare yourself for the challenges of the day, whether you are aware of them or whether they will take you by surprise. Build yourself up with words of affirmation. One affirmation I rely on daily is *Get Steady, Stay Steady.* This helps me to remember to keep pushing forward, stay on course, get back to basics, stay strong and grind it out. It helps me to remember that I know what I need to do to succeed. Another affirmation I rely on is *I can do all things in Christ who strengthens me.* This affirmation reminds me that, in times of weakness, doubt, or confusion, I can always rely on God to pull me through. It helps to me vertically align my thoughts.

I write affirmations on the same paper as my 10-10-10, in my car, around the house, and on my computer desktop. Throughout the day, I am reminded to stay focused on achieving my dreams. It is a way to give little moments of motivation and encouragement. It's like an energy drink for your spirit!

What then shall we say to this?
If God is for us, who can be against us?
~Rom. 8:31

I came so that they may have life and have it more abundantly.
~Jn. 10:10

Building the Habit

The most demanding goals in your 10-10-10 are going to be the ones which are habit-building, requiring the most discipline, self-motivation, and self-renewal, such as becoming 100% debt free. Chances are, however, these will be the most satisfying to complete and check off your list. Do not be disheartened if you find the process of accomplishing your goals comes with difficulty: *the greater the effort, the greater the prize.* This should be a motivation, not a deterrent. Legendary Notre Dame football coach Lou Holtz has said, "Without self-discipline, success is impossible, period." You must search out your own dreams and goals through positive habit-building, because they're not searching for you.

It is said that it takes 21 days to build a habit. If you have taken this structured path to achieving your dreams and goals seriously using E5, 10-10-10, Vertical Alignment, and words of affirmation, you will be convinced of this life-changing way of living. Actions become habits; habits build dreams. Only through the act of the will do things become accomplished. It is through good habits that we build not only our dreams and goals but also our character. Aristotle tells us, "Character is that which reveals moral purpose, exposing the class of things a man chooses or avoids." Your character is the only thing you bring to heaven when you die: what you've become, how you have built yourself into the best possible person you can be, the person God intended you to be.

There will be times when you miss a day: we are all human. You always have the ability to pick up where you left off. If you have missed five days in a row and feel that you have taken some steps backward in achieving your dreams and goals, give yourself a nudge to reactivate your motivation. Use words of affirmation to get you back on track. Ignite the desire within you to start walking forward again. Look at your Vertical Alignment and know that your dreams matter. It only takes one person to make a difference. Choose that person to be you—*you are worthy and your dreams count!*

Adding & Removing

When you have achieved one of your goals on your 10-10-10, it is good to replace it with another goal. This way, you allow yourself to be on a continuous pattern of personal growth and achievement. Put a line through the accomplished goal, but keep it in front of you, so that you can see your accomplishments and celebrate the victory! This gives you motivation and strength, knowing that you've won a battle and that you've grown and learned.

Removing a goal on your 10-10-10 can be difficult. You must ask yourself if this particular goal is really something worthy of a number on your 10-10-10. Is it a real dream, or is it simply something that belongs on your to-do list? For example, *I will re-assess our insurance companies and search for better rates.* This is not a life goal; it is a responsibility.

One of the goals on your 10-10-10 may just not sit right with you and you may realize that it is not the time to try to tackle this particular goal. Or it may be something you wished you could do in the past, but it's really not a part of your core dreams and goals. In other words, it's something you could live without.

If it is hard for you to discern what a core dream is and what is not, think to yourself, *at the end of my life, what will I desire to have accomplished?* This kind of question will put your list of dreams and goals in perspective and help you to weigh each listed goal in importance.

WRITING YOUR OWN 10-10-10

SELF Monetary

1._____

2._____

3._____

4._____

5._____

6._____

7._____

8._____

9._____

10._____

SELF Non-Monetary

1._____

2._____

3._____

4._____

5._____

6._____

7._____

8._____

9._____

10._____

OTHERS Monetary or Non-Monetary

1._____

2._____

3._____

4._____

5._____

6._____

7._____

8._____

9._____

10._____

Questions to Ask Yourself While Writing Your 10-10-10

Put some kick into the dream building process. Dreaming big dreams ignites the power of the child within you who isn't afraid to dream BIG! The bigger the dreams, the more you need God to help you, and the more miraculous the victories.

1. What are my spiritual needs/desires? My emotional needs/desires? My mental needs/desires? My physical needs/desires? My financial needs/desires?

2. What am I passionate about? When I have idle time, where does my mind wander (my desires)?

3. At the end of my life, what will I look back on and wish I had accomplished or be thankful for that I had accomplished?

4. What area of my life do I need to improve?

5. What is something I've always wanted to do?

6. What is it that always bothers me about my money situation?

7. Who is a person I've always wanted to help?

8. What is financially getting in the way of my dreams and goals?

9. What do I need to do to get to the next level of personal development?

10. How can I apply myself to help others with the use of my talents?

11. Do all of these goals fit within Vertical Alignment?

12. Are my goals possibilities? Are they motivated by proper desires? Are my goals and dreams in authority to God's laws and man's laws?

CHAPTER 5

Words of Affirmation: A Positive Outlook on Life

Consider it all joy (Jam. 1:2)

"God's on my team"

"You can do it!"

"Let go, let God"

"Get steady, stay steady"

"How do you eat an elephant? One bite at a time"

Words of affirmation are the words that give you the personal encouragement and confidence you need to achieve your goals and dreams. These words are important in your culture of thinking because *what you say is what you think, what you think is what you believe, and your belief controls your actions.* What this means is that if you truly believe in your dreams and goals, you will make it happen. Words of affirmation don't *teach* you to dream, but they help move you closer to your dreams and goals. You are training your mind through affirmations and the power of the spoken word to think as a dream maker. You are teaching yourself to weed out distractions—those things that prohibit you from going forward in your journey of success and fulfillment.

How do you displace negative thoughts? With positive thoughts! I've coached people who say things like: "I'm not that smart," and "I don't think I could do that." I tell them to change their words to: "I'm getting better at learning new things," and "I'll work at doing that." The term *glass half empty* is often used to describe someone who perpetually perceives life in a negative light. How hard is it, really, to see the glass half full? It is simply a mind set, a change in thought and attitude.

A very influential book in my journey with E5 has been *Self Love* by Robert Schuller. When I first read it, I was struck by the thought that, in my mind, I had hypnotized myself into negativity. What people had said to me, how people had treated me, and how I came to believe who I was, acted like a tainted set of glasses. The vision I had of myself was gray and bleak. This negativity would rub off on others through my words and actions. It affected my family life and my relationships with friends and at work. It hindered my ability to function at my greatest potential. Negativity that you harbor comes from deep within; it engrains itself into your inner being, and taints the world around you.

The moment of awareness of my negativity was a beautiful moment for me, because I was able to begin sowing seeds of positivity into my heart. I began to think of myself as worthy of my goals and my dreams, someone with dignity who was made by a God who thinks of me as a beautiful creation. I gained confidence and courage from this change in perspective, and I became a stronger person because of it.

Displacing negative thoughts with positive thoughts is an easy enough practice. On a physical level, we all practice this action often. We simply move the chair that is in our path. We move the car when it is prohibiting another vehicle from backing out of the driveway. This is a simple practice and an effective one. It is most effective to practice in our mind, which can be possessed by negativity on a regular basis, and which can lead us to a depressed, anxious state and destroy our belief system, in God's plan and in our ability to achieve the success we have worked hard to attain.

If losing 25 pounds is listed in your 10-10-10 under SELF, a bright sticky note on the refrigerator with the words, *You can do it!*, is a great way to keep yourself motivated and keep you believing in your power to control your thoughts and your actions. With this positive thinking, the prospect of reaching your goal will be much brighter.

Words of affirmation are personal motivators. Make them personal. Create your own. Find them in Scripture. Find the words that work best to instill confidence in yourself, help you strengthen your belief that you are a winner. With these words of affirmation, you have the ability to re-possess your thoughts and be the master of your domain.

Visible reminders to be positive and stay positive:

- Putting notes on your refrigerator, dash board, desktop, bedside table

- Keeping a note on your 10-10-10, on your agenda, on your Bible

- Writing on your bathroom mirror

AFFIRMATIVE GUIDELINES

There are two important reminders you must re-visit on a regular basis pertaining to positive decision-making as you face forks in the road in your everyday life:

1. If it doesn't positively influence my life in the next 2 to 5 years, don't think about it and don't do it.

2. If it doesn't move me closer to my dreams and goals (doesn't correlate with my 10-10-10 and Vertical Alignment), don't think about it and don't do it.

These two guidelines are considered your *affirmative guidelines*. They help you control the output of your actions. You ensure that the consequences of your actions are only positive, because your actions are all focused on creating good habits that lead to achieving your dreams and goals.

These affirmative guidelines are used as a tool to help you weed out wasteful experiences that will not propel you closer to your dreams and your goals.

- Is a one week vacation to Las Vegas with my friends leading me closer to my dreams and goals? Or would this be a distraction?

- Should I choose to use my entire Saturday to vegetate in front of the television or should I use this time to move forward in worthwhile projects?

I am not saying you cannot have fun! But you must earn it. *Pay now, play later*, is a way to look at it.

10-10-10, VERTICAL ALIGNMENT, WORDS OF AFFIRMATION, & THEIR RELATION TO BALANCE

And so, back to the overall achievement of living a life of balance: with your 10-10-10 written and in motion, your inner radar working in harmony with Vertical Alignment, your mind on a constant path of positivity, and a definite plan marked out for you to become the best possible person you can be, you will be achieving your life of balance between all five pillars (E5) of your human experience: spiritual longing, emotional complexities, high mental capacities, physical necessities, and financial realities.

But, now that I have explained the basics of balance and the tools that help us achieve balance and reach our dreams and goals, let us concentrate on what life really looks like with E5 balance. In essence, *what you desire your life to be.*

CHAPTER 6

Fruits of a Life of Balance

Better Relationship with God &
Better Knowledge of His Ways

A life of balance gives you a better knowledge of God because you are, to the best of your ability, living your life according to God's plan for you. You are living a life of discipline and virtue. You are building character and walking on the path that makes you the best person you can possibly be. This is what God wants of you. This, in itself, strengthens your relationship and bond with him, because you are on the same "wavelength."

This is not enough. To be on the same wavelength as your spouse, for example, does not build a loving, stable, lasting relationship in itself. It is only a sliver of what knowledge of, respect for, and love for each other really encompasses.

The spiritual discipline that you follow with honesty and integrity is the relationship-building time that makes a difference. This builds within you a peace within your heart with God, regardless of the bustle and distractions and noise of your daily life. In other words, you can live with inner serenity regardless of outer turmoil.

GOD IS THE ORIGIN

The fruits of a life of balance stem from God. Why? Because God gave you your body, your emotions, your heart, your mind, and everything that you are and that you possess. You have a responsibility to God in every aspect of your life: spiritual, emotional, mental, physical, and yes, even financial. He expects you to do this, and you have been anointed to do it for him and yourself. Responsibility in all five pillars of balance (E5) is, after all, spiritual, because it all derives from God. We all are meant to give back to him what he gave to us as a gift. *You are ready to build your life into something more productive and beautiful at a higher level.*

The fruit of faith is endless:

> *If you have faith the size of a mustard seed, you will say to this mountain, 'move from here to there,' and it will move. Nothing will be impossible for you.*
> ~Mt. 17:20-21

Faith gives you immense power, if you open yourself to Truth with a persistent and humble heart. Faith will allow you to see the world differently, as God is asking us to see it (with wisdom); it will give you hope, courage, strength, understanding and prudence, even in the face of adversity. These are godly virtues which will guide you through life and never lead you astray.

Better Knowledge of Self

When you are actively seeking a life of balance, you begin to better understand yourself through self-examination. This self-examination is a natural element of personal growth in seeking balance, and includes knowledge of your aspirations, knowledge of your strengths and weaknesses, and knowledge of your temperament and your love language.

DISCOVERING YOUR ASPIRATIONS THROUGH YOUR 10-10-10

The time and effort you put into discovering your aspirations is never wasted. After all, you can only fulfill your dreams by first knowing what they are.

Discovering Your Strengths and Your Weaknesses: Self-Mastery

By mastering something, you need to understand it and control it. It is liberating to discover your weaknesses and how you live off-balance, because only with this knowledge can you move towards improvement. Augustine of Hippo said, "This is the very perfection of a man, to find out his own imperfections." Pablo Picasso said, "I am always doing that which I cannot do in order that I may learn how to do it." It is only with this knowledge and acceptance of your weaknesses that you can begin to grow. Once you understand the areas that you are off-balance, you are able to work towards achievable goals. Step by step, you build habits through discipline to become a master of yourself.

Discovering your Temperament

In the beginning stages of being coached, I learned the value of understanding temperaments. This was a fascinating discovery for me. For the first time in my life I was beginning to understand why I acted the way I did. I began to clearly see the person that God created me to be, and it was both revealing and exciting. I began to understand my natural strengths and weaknesses within my temperament.

I also saw how these inclinations affected my goals, my relationships, and everything other part of my life. This was the biggest step for me as a student, because once I came to understand and accept my temperament, I could begin to build upon this foundation. I felt much more confident moving forward because of it.

Temperament is defined by Art and Larraine Bennett as "one aspect of an individual's total personality – the aspect related to behavior and reaction."[1] The four temperaments, or humors, have been taught since Plato. The basic concept is that each person has a system of hard-wiring that creates tendency, both in giving and in receiving, mentally and emotionally, which in turn affects the spiritual and physical aspects of that person. Your temperament is your natural inclinations toward ways of thinking and acting. It is important to know who you are because it helps you get a grip on how to reach equilibrium. Are you detailed, organized, methodical, or fun and happy-go-lucky? Are you empathetic to others' feelings? I will briefly detail each temperament (from excerpts in their book *The Temperament God Gave Your Spouse*), but primarily, I highly recommend that you read the Bennett's book *The Temperament God Gave You* for a comprehensive understanding of who you are in relation to your behaviors and reactions.

1. **Choleric Cheat Sheet**[2]

Responds	Quickly, intensely, with lengthy duration
Sociability	Extraverted; energized by social situations, but less talkative than the sanguine
Recognizable traits	Natural leadership and take-charge attitude; strong will; confident, opinionated, decisive, and competitive
Focus	Highly focused
Wants to know	The bottom line, the essentials, the action item
Makes decisions based on	Logic, expediency, and the goal (is willing to bend rules in favor of a successful outcome)
Needs	Loyalty, control, appreciation, independence; to be in charge
Weaknesses	Thinks his view is the best, the only right one; lacks empathy; fails to seek counsel; individualistic; bossy
During interpersonal conflict	Tends to blame others or get angry; insists on being right or wants to "fix it" immediately
Is annoyed/ upset by	Slowness, inefficiency, disloyalty, distractions, whiners, complainers
Pays attention to	Power, organizational chart, bottom line, success, goal
How to deal with the choleric	Treat with respect and admiration; allow him to take charge in appropriate ways; help him grow in empathy by showing him how it will help him become more successful

2. Sanguine Cheat Sheet[3]

Responds	Quickly, intensely, with short duration
Sociability	Extremely sociable, extraverted, attuned to what is going on around him (especially people)
Recognizable traits	Enthusiastic, lively, open talkative, social, creative, fun-loving, generous; greatly values relationship and people
Focus	Easily distracted, especially by externals; can be easily attracted to something new
Wants to know	Who will be there? Will it be fun? Are you going with me? Are you happy?
Makes decisions based on	Interpersonal connections; what other people think; who is involved; whether people will like them
Needs	Attention; fun activities together; positive interactions; flexibility; doing things together; joy in life
Weaknesses	Can be hasty or superficial; tends to flee from negative; scatterbrained; exaggerates; a finger in every pie; people-pleasing; lack of follow-through
During interpersonal conflict	Wants to look on the bright side; avoids negativity; may skim over problems or pretend everything's fine
Is annoyed/ upset by	Lack of attention; negativity or harsh comments, indifference or hostility; problems; lack of fun/love in life; anything boring or unpopular
Pays attention to	What people think about them; how things look; what is popular; what others think or do; what is "out there"
How to deal with the sanguine	Take a positive approach; do things together; express your love and affection for him; help him to set priorities and not over-book; help him to follow through; hold him accountable

3. Melancholic Cheat Sheet[4]

Responds	Slowly but intensely; a prolonged reaction, with intensity building over time
Sociability	Introverted; energy drained by social activities; needs time alone to recharge; is comfortable alone
Recognizable traits	Quiet, thoughtful, detailed, critical, high-minded, serious, sensitive, artistic, persevering, tends to "perfectionism"
Focus	Intense; inward; focused on detail; marked by persistence
Wants to know	More details and specifics; further information; what are the rules
Makes decisions based on	Principles, how things "ought" to be, the ideal
Needs	Support; help in initiating projects or social activities; to be heard and understood; order and quiet
Weaknesses	Slow to initiate; indecisive; can be critical and inflexible; will say no if pressed for immediate response
During interpersonal conflict	Tends to let problems build up and then will overstate or become awkwardly vehement and overly dramatic; tends to generalize negatively
Is annoyed/ upset by	Lack of principles; being rushed into decisions; frivolity; lack of attention to detail; superficiality; disrespect for personal order
Pays attention to	The ideal; internal feelings and thoughts; past grievances; procedures; what is "right"
How to deal with the melancholic	Respect their rules, their quiet, their order, and their space; support them in initiating; acknowledge their valuable insight into problems; give them time to make a decision; ask what is on their mind

4. **Phlegmatic Cheat Sheet**[5]

Responds	Slowly, not intensely, with short duration
Sociability	Easygoing, quiet, dependable, peacemaker, reserved, calm (especially in a crisis)
Recognizable traits	Quiet, reserved, easygoing, introverted, well-liked by many
Focus	Can be unmoved by externals, but can be distracted by internal feelings, especially those of discomfort
Wants to know	Will everything go smoothly? Are people getting along?
Makes decisions based on	Relationships; what others think or want; cooperation
Needs	Harmony, especially in interpersonal relations; structure; respect and appreciation; time for relaxation; peace
Weaknesses	Can lack initiative; overly compliant; might not stand up for self; overly tolerant of status quo
Is annoyed/ upset by	Interpersonal conflict, noise, chaos, intense or extreme behavior
During interpersonal conflict	Will take blame to avoid conflict; will outwardly acquiesce, but might internally withhold agreement; might avoid conflict altogether because anxiety is so acute
Pays attention to	What others think or want, cooperation, harmony, duty
How to deal with the phlegmatic	Encourage him to take charge; gentle reminders (never nag); give positive feedback and words of affirmation to build up his confidence

Have you gotten a feel for what your own temperament may be after reading these cheat sheets? Here is *A Quick Self-Test* that the Bennett's offer in their book:[6]

1. Sirens begin to whirl behind you and you realize that a police car is pulling you over. You think:

    ___ His radar gun is wrong. I was hardly speeding there must be some mistake the cars in front of me were speeding.

    ___ Oh no! I've heard of people getting arrested for this!

    ___ Was I driving fast? What's the speed limit on this road anyway?

    ___ Do I have my wallet? Where did I put the car registration?

2. You are on a silent retreat weekend. Your cell phone rings. What do you do?

    ___ You take the call it might be important. You are confident it won't impact things negatively.

    ___ I'm not going to answer. Don't they realize I am on a *silent* retreat? Why are they bothering me? They are so thoughtless!

    ___ You answer on the first ring and start chatting away. After all you've been silent too long already.

    ___ You don't want to disappoint the person on the other end, so you take the call, but whisper, so no one will hear.

3. Your boss asks you to come into his office. You think:

    ___ He has finally recognized my superior contributions. I'm getting a raise!

__ What's gone wrong *now*? I'll bet that new division manager has gotten caught in one of those schemes of his.

__ He probably likes my idea for the Christmas party theme.

__ I hope he doesn't want me to work late tonight...Oh well, I guess I'll have to stay...Sigh

The Bennetts explain the test results:

In each of those three items above, the first response is typical of the choleric temperament, the second melancholic, the third is sanguine, and the fourth phlegmatic. This short, humorous quiz illustrates the fundamental feature of the concept of temperament: people of different temperaments tend to respond to identical stimuli in very different ways. Furthermore, the way each person responds tends to be consistent throughout his life. This consistency or coherence of reaction is due to his temperament.[7]

DISCOVERING YOUR LOVE LANGUAGE

Soon after my study of temperaments, I began delving into the love languages through Dr. Gary Chapman's book *The Five Love Languages.* At first, I didn't understand how this was relevant to being coached on reaching my dreams and goals in life, but quickly realized that is it quite critical. The road to success is not a lonely journey: it is one filled with relationships that aid you along the way, relationships that strengthen you, and relationships that are pivotal to the attainment of your dreams. I couldn't be blind to the people around me who care about me, who help me, or who depend on me.

Dr. Gary Chapman has incredible insight on how we give and receive love. His book is an extremely useful guide for you in your quest to discover and achieve your dreams. Again, as I have done with the temperaments, I will briefly overview each love language as an aid to your personal discovery. This knowledge helps us with Vertical Alignment, which is all about relationships (relating to others). There are real ramifications in how we show our spiritual, emotional, and mental realities to others. Understanding your love language will be critical in achieving total balance vertically, spiritually, emotionally, mentally, physically, and financially.

Dr. Gary Chapman gives a brief description of each language of love:

1. **Words of Affirmation**

"Compliments, words of encouragement, and requests rather than demands all affirm the self-worth of [others]. They create intimacy, heal wounds, and bring out the full potential of [the other]."[8]

2. **Quality Time**

"Spending quality time together through sharing, listening, and participating in joint meaningful activities communicates that we truly care for and enjoy each other."[9]

3. **Receiving Gifts**

"Gifts are visual symbols of love, whether they are items you purchased or made, or are merely your own presence made available to [the other]. Gifts demonstrate that you care, and they represent the value of the relationship."[10]

4. **Acts of Service**

"Criticism of [another's] failure to do things for you may be an indication that 'acts of service' is your primary love language. Acts of service should never be coerced but should be freely given and received, and completed as requested."[11]

5. **Physical Touch**

"Physical touch, as a gesture of love, reaches to the depths of our being. As a love language, it is a powerful form of communication from the smallest touch on the shoulder to the most passionate kiss."[12]

What are your love languages? How about the love languages of your spouse or your children? On Dr. Gary's website www.5lovelanguages.com he offers a quick test that could help you determine your love language and begin your journey to understanding yourself and others around you. We offer his questions here for you:[13]

- ☐ I feel especially loved when people express how grateful they are for me, and for the simple, everyday things I do.

- ☐ I feel especially loved when a person gives me undivided attention and spends time alone with me.

- ☐ I feel especially loved by someone who brings me gifts and other tangible expressions of love.

- ☐ I feel especially loved when someone pitches in to help me, perhaps by running errands or taking on my household chores.

- ☐ I feel especially loved when a person expresses feelings for me through physical contact.

If you check-marked:

> Statement one: Words of Affirmation is your primary love language

> Statement two: Quality Time is your primary love language

> Statement three: Gifts is your primary love language

> Statement four: Acts of Service is your primary love language

> Statement five: Physical Touch is your primary love language

To have a comprehensive understanding of each love language, it is imperative to read Dr. Gary's book. This will be a great tool to a greater understanding of yourself and others around you.

Better Knowledge of Others

With the power and knowledge that you obtain through (E5) balance, you can help others to find out their own personalities and talents and to develop them as leaders. Imagine the possibilities when you have become proficient in figuring out others' love languages and temperaments. You can learn how to better work with individuals as a team to efficiently and effectively accomplish goals by utilizing their strengths and preferences. Jesus is a perfect example of a leader who used his wisdom and power to reach out to others through instruction and action. He calls us to do the same.

As a leader, I have many volunteers working under me. My way of motivating them, appreciating them, and lifting them up to be the best that they can be, is to pinpoint their love languages and temperaments. I give the Sanguines roles of hospitality, the

Melancholics roles of organization, the Cholerics roles that appeal to their need to take hold of the reigns and run with our goals in mind, and the Phlegmatics I count on to steady the group, acting as an anchor for the team.

I am most particular in learning others' love languages so that I can best show them my appreciation for their volunteering. One particular volunteer I work with who is very motivated and whom I can always count on, is a sensitive soul who takes others' words to heart. In other words, his primary love language is Words of Affirmation. I am always careful when I have a critique, to bolster it with an affirmation of the role he plays as a volunteer. This simple act of sensitivity towards another's love language raises him up to another level; it shows him that I care about him as a person, that he is more than a warm body helping out, and that he is of value and worth. Being sensitive to others' love language can help them achieve greatness, because their sense of worth is upheld, which motivates them to be the best people they can be.

Peace & Equilibrium

When all things are in order in your house, you have a sense of peace. E5 allows you to have better focus at work, give more attention to your spouse and children, and, in all areas of life, be more attentive and insightful. You can give yourself fully to the task at hand. You are not internally split because of stressful worries pulling you away mentally and emotionally.

Our world is full of anxiety because its philosophy revolves around the ego. The prevailing belief of *relativism* that dominates the mind of our culture, vocalized in such sayings as, "if it makes you happy, than it must be okay," or "to each his own," takes from our consciences the sense of responsibility for our brothers and sisters and belief that there is a definite Right and Wrong and a definite Truth to adhere our lives to. *Hedonism*, the belief that pleasure is the greatest good and should be sought at all costs, is an ego-building machine that completely revolves around the senses instead of what is Good and True. Our media's propagation of *individualism*, the ultimate concern for the Self (predominating over God and others) is massacring all sense of community and family. When your Self is put at the center of your world, you are left feeling alone and heavy with the responsibilities of your world; after all, you are not a god! You cannot carry and conquer on your own.

Peace also reigns when you know that everything has its time and place and you control when and how you deal with each demand in your life. For example, when you are living Vertical Alignment properly, you are giving your full self to what is in front of you. When you sit to eat dinner with your family in the evening, you are focused on the conversation, the stories, and actions and the relationships around the table. You are contributing to the experience. You are able to do so because you know that your complete focus will be given to other demands later on.

THE THREE POWERS

The Three Powers are invaluable habits that propel you to achieve your dreams and your goals. Each of these three powers helps you to achieve balance, and live with passion and purpose.

1. **Power of Submission: United to Christ (Make Him First Priority Through Vertical Alignment)**

The Power of Submission is the total union with God that includes *trust and loving, respectful obedience* to his Will. You are smaller than God; he is greater than you. You, therefore, allow him to lead you. Just as a Private in the army, you allow your General to lead you. This does not mean that you cannot be a leader yourself, but that you are ultimately under his command.

Understand "submission" as being *sub*, or secondary, to the *mission*. In all areas of your life, you play roles of Leader or Follower. In everything you do, whether it be work or play, you always have a goal set before you, and in attaining that goal, you are either the leader or the one being led, the submissive one. It is natural to us as human beings to follow rules set out for us, to submit to them. Whether it be stopping at a stop sign (man's law), or adhering to the commandment *You shall not steal* (God's law), it is part of our makeup to abide by certain rules that we perceive to be good for us, that protect us. The success principals we have laid out will require you to submit your ego, to be open minded to change. Only then can change come about.

2. Power of Unity: You Live Your Faith to Complete Your Goals

The Power of Unity is the power that comes from being united to God in his will, and united to others with whom you have meaningful relationships, especially within the living of Vertical Alignment. In other words, *Love Unites.*

Love is Patient, Love is Kind.
It is not jealous, it is not pompous,
It is not inflated, it is not rude,
It does not seek its own interests, it is not quick-tempered,
It does not brood over injury,
It does not rejoice over wrongdoing but rejoices with the truth.
It bears all things, believes all things,

Hopes all things, endures all things.
~1 Corinthians 13:4-7

For instance, if your 16 year old son tells you, "I hate you; you have let me down," or your spouse says one evening, "You've disappointed me; you can sleep on the couch tonight," these breakdowns in relationships break down your balance and affect your mental toughness that lead you to achieve your goals and dreams. Unity within your relationships ensures a realm of harmony, charity, and peace because you are loving others and showing them your appreciation for their presence in your life through your servitude. It ensures a more joyful, peaceful life which leads to a greater focus on your dreams and goals.

Unity is a sign of strength. To be unified in a common purpose creates a bond that can stand through trials and tribulations. Unity is the cohesive thread that binds together the tapestry of a family, a church, an organization, or any type of group. I recently had to deal with disharmony in my organization as a result of a clashing of personalities and interests. This lack of unity immediately made an impact on the strength of our team: we were less effective in our productivity. Drive and confidence was down. As the leader, I had to carefully take in mind the temperaments and love languages of the parties in mind while I set about settling the situation tactfully. I had a personal conversation with each of my team members, building them up with positive reinforcement, redefining with clarity my expectations, and sending them off with a renewed positive outlook on our mission as a team. Only then could I re-instill the harmony, charity, and peace by re-uniting our interests and goals.

Jesus has told us that when two or more are gathered in his name, he is present (Mt. 18:20). When you are united to him in your desires and will, he provides the path to attain your dreams and goals. No dream or goal is attainable alone. A true dream takes the people God puts in your path to help you along the way, to give you encouragement, advice, and support. Unity must be upheld in order to rise to your potential. There are no lone rangers in dream building.

> *At the end of our life we shall be judged by charity.*
> *~John of the Cross*

3. **Power of the Spoken Word: Bring Your Goals into Existence Through Your Words Which Give Power**

You are powerful even when you are powerless. The words you speak, no matter who you are, what your status, where you live, have the power to create or to destroy.

I was the baby of the family, the joker, who was good for a laugh. I didn't excel in much except sports, mostly because (I now realize with hindsight) I was not encouraged in much more than that, since my attention span was short and my grades in school didn't come easily. No one saw much potential in me. As a result, *I* didn't believe in me.

It took *one person* who believed in me and spoke that belief into me often, and this changed my world: the way I saw myself, the way I saw my future, and the way I approached life. My life now is the result of the Positive Power of the Spoken Word.

An inspiring story of the power of the spoken word is the success story of sales legend, Frank Bettger. Frank grew up in Philadelphia around the turn of the twentieth century. Frank's formal education was limited to a few years of schooling. His father died when he was still quite young, and he was forced to work in order to help his mother support the family, which included five children.

He woke up at the crack of dawn to sell newspapers. At age 14 he left school to be a steamfitter's helper.

In his late teens, Frank became a professional baseball player in a Tri-State League for Johnstown, PA. Despite the great increase in pay, there was something missing—something that Frank did not recognize, but that his manager noticed, and had him fired because of it. Disillusioned, he asked his manager why he was fired. The words his manager spoke would change Frank's life from there on out: "Frank... Whatever you do after you leave here, for heaven's sake, wake yourself up, and put some life and enthusiasm into your work!"[14]

Enthusiasm! Something clicked with Frank. He chose to take his manager's words to heart, and began to approach his career with enthusiasm. With those words ringing in his ears, Frank worked himself enthusiastically out of the $25 a month Atlantic League right into the major leagues.

Two short years as a major leaguer, in a game versus the Chicago Cubs, Frank injured his arm so badly that he was forced to give up the game of baseball at the tender age of 29. He went back to Philadelphia and began to sell life insurance. Frank was an utter failure at selling. Desperate for money, he figured that he would give up sales and would apply to be a shipping clerk. Even as a shipping clerk, he realized he had to overcome his fear of speaking in public, so he enrolled himself in a Dale Carnegie training course in public speaking. During his presentation one night in class, Frank's lack of enthusiasm caught Carnegie's attention. Carnegie then gave a riveting talk on enthusiasm that caught Frank's attention. He began to equate his lack of enthusiasm with underachievement, not only on the baseball field but also in every other area of his life, including selling. Frank explains, "The very fault which had threatened to wreck my career in baseball was now threatening to wreck my career as a salesman."[15]

From that moment on, Frank decided to stick with selling insurance and put some enthusiasm into it. That decision led him to success and fame, all because of the simple but powerful words of two men who encouraged him to add enthusiasm to his tasks. These words Frank took to heart and spoke to himself. He believed them and put them into action.[16]

If Frank's manager or Dale Carnegie had chosen to speak negative, harmful words to Frank (*Frank, you just don't have it together,* or *Frank, you just don't excel in this; go try something else*), Frank would have continued the cycle of failure in all that he did. Likewise, if these two men would have chosen to say nothing at all, and watch Frank wane in his apathetic approach to his tasks, Frank would never have reached fulfillment and success as he did.

Our words are powerful, both the words we speak to others and the words we speak to ourselves. It is known, for example, that large numbers of children who stutter have been found to have at least one parent who speaks often with harsh, demeaning, or threatening tones. Believe in the power of your words that you possess. Be responsible and tender with it. *You have the power to create or to destroy.*

PART 2

The 5 Balances of Life

The path to success requires a strategic plan. Like every board game or competition, there are tactics that will get you to the end victorious. Within this section, you will find the strategies and methods, knowledge you must internalize and habits you must develop, to win. You are making the journey on the path to success ....

CHAPTER 7

Spiritual Balance

Give yourself fully to God. He will use you to accomplish great things on the condition that you believe much more in his love than in your own weakness.

~ *Mother Teresa of Calcutta*

Let your religion be less of a theory and more of a love affair.

~*G.K. Chesterton*

It is this spiritual freedom—which cannot be taken away—that makes life meaningful and purposeful.

~*Victor Frankl*

Father Maximilian Kolbe sat in the dark, dingy bunker with
a genuine smile and aura of joy and peace. His body, emaci-
ated and starved, ached from the months of torture spent at the
Auschwitz concentration camp. These were his last days.

At first glance, he looked small, insignificant, withered in defeat.
But his fellow prisoners knew differently. He was a man who
chose death so that a fellow prisoner with a wife and children
could live. He was a man who trusted in God so deeply that no
vile conditions, scare tactics, and torture could take away his
inner freedom. He would pray, sing hymns, and raise up the
hearts of those around him, all of whom knew they were liv-
ing their last days on earth. He never asked for anything, never
complained. His compassion extended even to the SS soldiers,
his torturers who prided themselves in such inhumanity. Their
contempt for him turned to utter frustration because they could
not take away the one thing they prided themselves in stealing
from all of their prisoners: the life within them.

The relationship Kolbe shared with God was undeniable. He was
confident in it. He lived for it. He brought others to God's comfort
and peace even amidst the harshest conditions of ignominy, de-
privation, and despair. The goodness brought forth from his faith,
hope, and love, was irrefutable even to the nonbelievers.

What is Spirituality?

I myself will be the shepherd of my sheep.
~Ezekiel 34:15

The spiritual life is God's relationship with you, your relation-
ship with God, and your continuous efforts to make this rela-
tionship more authentic and more genuine.

In order to become spiritually balanced, a comprehensive under-standing of what the spiritual life fully entails is necessary.

The spiritual life is a calling, a path "to be holy and without blem-ish before him" (Eph. 1:5). This may seem like an unrealistic, un-attainable, perhaps undesirable, goal to reach for. But what this really means, in modern words we can all understand and all hope for, is to *become the person we were created and intended to be.* Pope John Paul II has challenged us with these simple yet deeply wise words: "Become what you are!" We are children of God, spir-itual beings, with overwhelming capacities to be great. What an exciting journey, to discover and develop your talents, which may be hidden, untapped treasures!

God desires you to know him, to love him and to be like him in all things. Why would a perfect and Supreme Being want anything less? He wants you to live a joyful and fulfilling life, and he offers you every opportunity to reach that joy and fulfillment. You sim-ply have to accept.

How do you accept God's love and generosity? By becoming the best person you can possibly be; by living your one life in the fullest possible way; by living with passion for what is good and true and real. God's gift to each of us, regardless of race, color, or creed is our very life. Our gift back to him is what we do with our life.

GOD WITH US

God's relationship with us has been wounded as a result of our pride. The human inclination to think first of ourselves has gotten us into a lot of trouble! We tend to look to ourselves for guid-ance and inspiration and therefore lose our close connection with the One that holds the key to all things. Thankfully, like any good Father would do, he has a plan to restore a relationship with us, to bring us back to communion with himself. In other words, *God all along has desired for us to be in balance: in balance with himself and in life.*

I will not leave you orphans, I will come to you.

~Jn. 14:18

God asks us to be his adopted sons and daughters through Jesus Christ. He knows how to act as a parent. We need to learn how to become exemplary children. Because of God's desire to be close to us, he has given us his spirit, to teach us and guide us through life. St. Paul writes, "If we live by the Spirit, let us also walk by the Spirit" (Gal 5:25). In essence, the spiritual life is a life energized and led by the Spirit in the quest of holiness (becoming the best person we can possibly be).

...my yoke is easy, and my burden light.

~Mt. 11:30

Life is full of suffering and loss. You know people who suffer from (or you have suffered yourself from) stress, anxiety, divorce, fear, worry, doubt, and so many other burdens that are a part of life. Without understanding the spiritual life, we all feel burdened and lost. *The inevitability of situations that create suffering is precisely why your life demands balance and spiritual renewal.*

TRUE FREEDOM, TRUE HAPPINESS, & THE QUESTION OF SUFFERING

*If there is a meaning in life at all, then
there must be a meaning in suffering.
Suffering is an ineradicable part of life, even as fate and death.
Without suffering and death, human life cannot be complete.*

~Victor Frankl

Although the world is full of suffering, it is also full of overcoming.

~Helen Keller

*God had one Son on earth without sin,
but never one without suffering.*

~Augustine of Hippo

True freedom, in the words of Pope John Paul II, "consists not in doing what we like, but in having the right to do what we ought." He speaks with utter certainty, not simply out of belief, but out of experience. Karol Wojtyla was witness to the deepest sufferings of man during the Second World War in Poland. He worked in the rock mines during the day and secretly studied for the priesthood at night. He led an underground theatre company to help bring happiness to the lives of his fellow countrymen who were in the thick of the repression and degradation of Nazi command.

Americans take for granted the rights and privileges we are granted. Most of us have never experienced a life where freedom to live according to your conscience and right judgment is taken away. Many of us have lived our whole lives with the *choice* to hold fast to or squander our dignity. Taking our rights and privileges for granted has undoubtedly played a role in our misunderstanding of what true freedom entails. The inner freedom that results from doing what you *should do* is a freedom that consists of serenity, hope for all things good, and confidence in yourself and in God's Will for your life.

True Happiness is an interior disposition of peace and joy that comes from being right with God and right with your self, as only God has intended for you, specifically and uniquely. Happiness comes from the interior knowledge that you are living with virtue and character and working to becoming the best possible person you can be.

The question still begs to be answered: how can I experience true freedom and true happiness amidst all the suffering in this world? There is unrelenting human suffering in today's world, an undeniable suffering we all experience through poverty, sickness, death, war, injustice, imprisonment, and violence. One of the biggest hang-ups people have today about *God*, his justice, his equality, and his love, has to do with suffering. In fact, the same hang-up crosses borders into the realm of *happiness*: many of you do not believe you can achieve it because of suffering. Accordingly, *success* is given a bad rap and deemed unattainable because of a lack of hope and experience of hardship or suffering. How often have you heard such phrases as, "well, not everyone can have it all," or, "It's obvious God has preferences in this world," or even, "Some people are just dealt a bad hand."

There are people today, people who live in poverty, with sickness, in war-torn countries, wrongfully imprisoned, violated and degraded, who live with joy and peace, and fulfillment. This may be hard to believe, but they are living proofs that t*he achievability of peace and joy amidst such uncontrollable circumstances is attainable.* We were all called to play the "hand we were dealt" with great enthusiasm.

Helen Keller has said, "Although the world is full of suffering, it is also full of overcoming." In the 2010 Documentary *The Human Experience*, a group of young men decide to travel into different parts of the world and experience life with the poor, the sick, the homeless, and the rejected. One particular visit was to a leper colony in India. There, they meet the most dilapidated humans they had ever encountered: blind, missing limbs, deformities ransacking their bodies. Amidst such disfigurement and suffering, they encountered a blind and withered man who was the pillar of hope and joy in the community. He tells the young men the story of his rejection, of how his own son had denounced him. His physical condition is worthy of grievance. And yet, this man had a choice to live in misery or to live the remainder of his life with joy for his blessings, namely the blessing of community among the lepers in the colony. *He overcame his circumstances of utter dejection and abandonment and chose to rejoice in communion, joy, and being a strength for others.*

Applicable Spirituality: Abiding by Truth

Pope John Paul II is a universally-respected 20th century genius whose mind and faith merits respect from all faith vantage points. He has stated that, "Although each individual has the right to be respected in his own journey in search of the truth, what comes first and foremost is our moral obligation to abide by the truth once we have found it" (Veritatis Splendor, 34). This is important to our discussion because we can only find spiritual balance if we are living with honesty and integrity in our relationship with God. In other words, once we know what is true and what is of God, we must adhere to it. This gives us balance.

But, to bring this down to a day-by-day focus, we have to learn how to make God's Truth and his relationship with us applicable.

Applying our faith to our everyday lives is what most of us find to be challenging. It is easier to push aside time alone in prayer than to push aside our physical necessities such as eating and sleeping, or to push aside the demands of our job or responsibilities that we are held accountable to by others.

Only God can save us from ourselves; nevertheless, God expects us to cooperate, and it is in this cooperation that you and I discover our true greatness. Our greatness is realized as a result of our response to God's love. We discover our talents by discovering our Selves, and we discover our Selves by discovering God.

It takes a person with strong character, courage, values, and morals to adhere to a lifelong commitment to Truth. God knows whether or not you or I are holding up our ends of the bargain. Family and friends, likewise, will know your virtue and character through your words and actions, "...for the tree is known by its fruits" (Mt 12:33).

Why do I need a Spiritual life? (What's in it for me?)

When you let go and let God into your life, you become God-Powered. Your spirit is uplifted, strengthened, and protected. You are given gifts that this world can't give you: wisdom, understanding, counsel, fortitude, knowledge, piety, and fear of the Lord. Most importantly, God will guide you to achieve your goals in life. He created you, your heart, your desires, your dreams... and so, he knows what you truly desire, what your purpose is, and what you need for a fulfilling life. Like any good friend, go to him for advice and counsel. After all, he is omniscient and all-powerful!

I am aware that each one of us is at a different place in our spiritual journeys. Some believe that the spiritual realm does not have much to do with your daily life. There are some of you who feel like a day without praying is like a day without food or drink: you're starving for some sustenance. Others are somewhere in between. Perhaps you believe in the importance of God's presence in your life, but have not yet succeeded in finding a good balance between the spiritual and the temporal within your day-by-day reality. Some of you may not put much emphasis at all on your spiritual wellbeing, and may not yet understand how God works in your life at all, or why this is pertinent to your lifestyle.

This is why I have decided to come at the spiritual life from two points of view. I would like to talk first about the benefits of living with a spiritual sense from a very worldly point of view, meaning that even an atheist could understand the benefits of believing in and worshiping God. Secondly, I will discuss with you the benefits of living with a spiritual sense from a believer's point of view.

Benefits of Living with a Spiritual Sense from a Non-Believer's Point of View

If you come at spirituality from a purely logical point of view, without any regard for faith, you would still understand that living with faith in God and adherence to him is beneficial to your wellbeing, and that Spiritual Balance plays an integral role in the balance of your whole Person. Let's visit some of the logical explanations for choosing a life of spiritual integrity:

- **It's a Win-Win Situation:** "If you place [your bet] with God, you lose nothing, even if it turns out that God does not exist. But if you place it against God, and you are wrong and God does exist, you lose everything." ~Peter Kreeft

- **Longer and Happier Life:** Studies have shown that people who attend church tend to live longer lives and happier lives. The link between faith and health has not been conclusive in these studies, except to hypothesize that belonging to a community gives people hope and an outlet for stress, and helps to bring a sense of meaning into people's lives.

- **Meaningful and Purposeful Life:** 55% of Americans "find meaning and purpose for their lives from their faith. For the spiritually committed, it is not wealth, position, power, or even the pursuit of the American Dream that gives their lives meaning; that meaning is derived from their faith." ~Albert L. Winseman

- **Live in Faith and Hope (not doubt or fear):** A person of faith lives with hope for the future and with peace about the outcome of their lives. If you are confident about your relationship with God, you will have peace about your death and the death of others you love.

- **Builds Character:** Living a life of faith gives you a moral compass in which to live by, which builds character, virtue, and principles of leadership. In *Mere Christianity*, C.S. Lewis says, "All that we call human history—money, poverty, ambition, war, prostitution, classes, empires, slavery—[is] the long terrible story of man trying to find something other than God which will make him happy."

- **Builds Leadership Savvy:** Living by the success principles of the Christian faith gives you the edge on leadership because you are less egocentric and more in tune with the needs of others.

- **It can do no harm:** "One of the few things in life that can-not possibly do harm in the end is the honest pursuit of the truth." ~Peter Kreeft

Benefits of Living with a Spiritual Sense from a Believer's Point of View

> *We can't believe what we believe to be untrue,*
> *and we can't love what we believe to be unreal.*
>
> *~Peter Kreeft*

- **You are a Role Model:** When living a life of peace, hope, harmony, and faith, benefits of spiritual balance, you are a natural role model for others who see a confidence and peace about you that they admire. Your children, family, friends, and acquaintances want to emulate you because they recognize that you possess enviable characteristics.

- **Power and Strength Through God:** In moments of weakness or hardship, you are able to call on God and his power to give you strength and clarity to carry on without becoming imbalanced and thrown off your goal-oriented path.

- **Comfort Amidst Trials:** Victor Frankl in *Man's Search for Meaning* suggests that the Holocaust prisoners with a good relationship with God were "able to retreat from their terrible surroundings to a life of inner riches and spiritual freedom." Jesus tells us, "I will not leave you orphans; I will come to you" (Jn. 14:18). You are able to talk to God, and find emotional and spiritual equilibrium through prayer. Most of us will not suffer as a Prisoner of War, however it is important to know that *overcoming* is for all of us, no matter how great or small the trials in life. All trials, when upon us, are just as big as anyone else's.

- **Trust in Providence:** Through his Providence, God brings people into your life. With faith, you are able to trust that God is working alongside you as you put your best foot forward to succeed. And, despite success or failure, you can believe that all situations are in God's hands. With this awareness of God's plan and your role in it, you also become aware of how you are a part of history because God is the author of history. You can understand that you play a bigger role than you may be able to comprehend. "History is a story written by the finger of God." ~C.S. Lewis

How to Apply Spiritual Balance

SELF-KNOWLEDGE: TEMPERAMENT & LOVE LANGUAGE

A powerful tool to achieving spiritual balance in your life is to understand yourself in an all-encompassing way. Namely, your temperament plays a big role in the way you approach prayer and your relationship with God. Learn to cater to your temperament's strengths and curb your natural distractions for the sake of spiritual growth. In other words, know who you are, how God made you as a unique individual.

At one point when my wife and I were dating, she was driving a manual Toyota Corolla. I lived at the end of a cul-de-sac, and would take her car for a drive, back and forth on my street, to get the hang of the stick shift. At first, the whole experience was plain scary: stalling, screeching, and jerking were all part of the driving experience. But I quickly became a smoother driver, and soon enough, she agreed to let me drive her around on our dates. I had learned a new skill, and with that knowledge came control and agility.

Even though I considered myself a seasoned driver with my experience in an automatic, I had to begin again, by learning and understanding the workings of a manual car. Applied to life, this example can be helpful: once we learn and understand our own selves, we are able to skillfully use this knowledge to steer through life's challenges. For example:

- A sanguine might find that charitable work is a great way to strengthen his spiritual muscles.

- A choleric may find that she needs to schedule that 15 minutes of prayer time into the self-inflicted busyness of her day.

- A reflective melancholic may find that building a spiritual life is second nature, enjoying the reflective nature of his conversations with God, but needs to learn to ease up on his legalistic approach to religious practice.

- An easy-going phlegmatic will benefit from a scheduled time for prayer, and will check off the "task" with enthusiasm.

When you begin to understand your temperament, you will find that you can reach an understanding of the whys and hows of your inclinations and desires within your everyday world.

Applying your love language to God is equally important in your spiritual journey. After all, living a spiritual life means that you are in a living relationship with God. God understands all love languages and is equally content with any way you show your genuine love for him. He knows your needs and desires and what love language you speak. Your job is to apply your needs and desires to this spiritual relationship. Why? *Because you respond to both the receiving and the giving of love.* In other words, showing affection is just as important in a relationship as is receiving affection from another.

How will you show your affection and appreciation for God? If your primary love language is Words of Affirmation, make sure that words of homage to God play a prominent role in your prayer. If your love language is Gifts, offer God the gifts of your time, your tithing to charities, or even a self-offering, giving him all that you do during the day. If your love language is quality time, you will feel that you are offering yourself fully by setting aside a concrete time for prayer each day. Our emotions are an integral part of who we are, and cannot be dismissed in our prayer life. Therefore, if we respond to our relationship with God the way that we would want to be shown love, we will experience emotional fulfillment on a deeper, spiritual level.

ALIGNING YOUR GOALS WITH GOD'S: VERTICAL ALIGNMENT & 10-10-10

Vertical Alignment demands that you are a "man for others"— that you live a life of servitude to others and God through your time, treasure, talent, abilities, and attitude. You and I could easily put a list of goals together that are self-serving, but if we connect the 10-10-10 with the Vertical Alignment, the Vertical Alignment helps us to see what in our 10-10-10 is self-seeking and should be taken out of our list. For example, on Monetary Self, you may have written "I want to buy myself a new class ring." What good is this goal bringing to you and to others? This would be a self-seeking goal that is not a difference-maker. However, a goal such as, "I want a new truck to replace the old beat-up junker" may sound self-seeking, but you know that a newer truck would represent your company more attractively, which, in turn, both supports your family and keeps them safer on the road.

God works through you. He places desires in your heart for you to write down in your 10-10-10, to look at, and to accomplish it. A desire could be helping a friend, something that gives you spiritual fulfillment as well as giving your Self for the good of others. God's desires for you can be recognized by a deep yearning in your heart you suddenly feel when you meet someone who is needy, to put your time, treasure, and talent into helping in the best way you can, keeping within your Vertical Alignment while fulfilling this particular goal to the utmost. Vertical Alignment can be used to gauge the desires of the heart to aid you in creating goals on the 10-10-10 in all three areas, Self Monetary, Self Non-Monetary, and Others.

It is important to have that connection with God, to be prayerful and virtuous, because he places that agape-love, the servanthood, within your desires, which is the carrier of goodwill in the world that propels you toward holiness.

FLEXIBILITY & TRUST

1. **Willingness to "Let Go & Let God"**

In the evening before Peter walked on water, he didn't think that he would be capable of participating in a miracle. While in his fishing boat with the other Apostles, a few miles off shore, tumultuous waves hit from all sides. Suddenly they all saw the silhouette of Jesus against the horizon, walking towards them on the water.

They were terrified by this but, for a moment, Peter's heart was lifted and he felt that he could accomplish anything. With Jesus' command, he stepped out onto the waves and began to walk toward his Master. This was a moment of complete confidence and trust in God. His eyes were on Jesus. He walked assertively upon the waves.

Whenever you are striving to be the best that you can be, striving to reach dreams and goals that seem beyond your reach (but within your talents), it takes a supernatural trust to say, "Listen God. I can't do this alone. But with you I can. I don't know how I can balance seven ministries, a family, a book, a 10-10-10, meeting with people in prison, but I know that you can help me." Trusting in God is a way to let go of yourself and know that, ultimately, God is going to work through you to accomplish what he desires.

...for God, all things are possible.
~Mt. 19:26

It took one moment of doubt for Peter to start sinking. But not all was lost: Jesus reached out and grabbed him from drowning. We all have our moments of doubt. But we must pick ourselves back up and shake the tumultuous waves from their grasp around our feet. God is always there to pick us back up and help us continue on our journey. John Maxwell has written an entire book on "failing forward," meaning that we can use our failings as instruments of experience that participate in our growth as an individual and teach us wisdom.

2. Taking Control

The goal of being spiritually balanced is to let God be the sole proprietor of your heart. There is a simple prayer I learned as a child that has helped me to visualize my heart as a place only for God:

Lord, teach me that I may be a little house that's fit for thee.

A house of shining window panes,
clean from all smears and smuts and stains.

No blinds drawn darkly down to hide
the things that lie and lurk inside

and creep and mutter in the night, for honesty is clear as light.

So I will take my broom and clear
every dishonest thought and fear

and deed right out that I may be a little house that's fit for thee.

Virtuous control and possessive control are two very different attitudes. When you become spiritually docile to God's Will, you don't lose your own will and lose all control, but you "consult" with God before making any decisions. He still allows you to take the wheel. That is free will.

Benefits of Spiritual Balance

Awareness of a Spiritual Reality

Finally, draw your strength from
the Lord and from his mighty power.

Put on the armor of God so that you may be able
to stand firm against the tactics of the devil.

~Eph. 6:10-11

Living with a deeper sense of *true* reality, which encompasses the spiritual realm, gives you a greater sense of purpose and meaning. The natural human thirst for meaning is quenched with the awareness of God's existence and love for you. He holds the answers to life's basic and persistent questions, and our only job is to respond to his love.

In today's world we are often caught in a reality that masks us from the spiritual realm: materialism, individualism, stresses and frustrations, the daily grind. It is easy to be caught in this web without giving ourselves the time for replenishment through quiet, peace, and prayer. Our world alone has nothing to give us; if we allow ourselves to be consumed by it, it will drown us with anxiety resulted from the daily grind.

> *We need to find God, and he cannot*
> *be found in noise and restlessness.*
>
> *God is the friend of silence. See how nature*
> *- trees, flowers, grass- grows in silence;*
>
> *see the stars, the moon and the sun, how they move in silence...*
>
> *We need silence to be able to touch souls.*
>
> *~Teresa of Calcutta*

Strength of Character through Submission & Sacrifice

Spirituality gives us the strength that builds our character. Character is the only thing we take with us when we die. None of us are getting out of this life alive; we are all going to die! This reality can fill us with fear and cause us to cower or it can boost our trust in God and propel us to live closer to the spiritual realm. It is through the power of submission that we begin to understand and grasp the spiritual reality because we come to know that God is ultimately above us. He is bigger than us; he has more control than we do.

Being spiritually balanced gives us the ability to live, as it is said, with our feet planted firmly on the ground and our eyes looking to heaven. In other words, the spiritual realm has a place in your life, and you allow God to be the center of your choices and decisions through the use of Vertical Alignment.

If you want to be the best Kung Fu fighter in the world, you will search out the Master Teacher. Under his guidance and teaching, you will undoubtedly excel. You will not leave his Mentorship with a Green Belt, but instead you will have reached your highest potential with the best moves and secrets the Master imparts, with a Black Belt tied around your waste.

In reference to God: when you allow yourself to be trained, taught, and motivated by the greatest Coach ever imagined, don't you think you will come to learn the best of the best? You will learn to be great from the Greatest of all. If you let him, he will teach you. *Let go and let God.*

Submit yourself to God, and sacrifice your comfort for the greater good. As it is said in the sports world, *no pain, no gain.* Or, more eloquently said:

> *...we also glory in our sufferings, because*
> *we know that suffering produces*
>
> *perseverance; perseverance, character; and*
> *character, hope. And hope does not put*
>
> *us to shame, because God's love has been*
> *poured out into our hearts through the*
>
> *Holy Spirit, who has been given to us.*
>
> *~Rom. 5:3-5*

PEACE

This understanding should not fill us with fear but should bring us comfort and peace. Trust in God is vitally important if we are to take this way of life seriously, living according to Vertical Alignment and living to reach our highest potential in life. If we are caught in the web of the world, we don't come to this understanding of our need for God. We think clothes, food, entertainment, and even family and friends, can fulfill us completely. But without the spiritual realm piercing our reality, we are left with an emptiness that we cannot fill with worldly goods.

Personal Experience of Spiritual Balance

Mark's Experience:

I did not attain spiritual balance at baptism or through my conversion to Catholicism; there was a very specific date on which it all clicked together for me. This date was June 6, 2000. I was meeting with one of my mentors and he asked me if I was living life in *victory and power* or in *agony and defeat.* I admitted to him honestly that I was in defeat. He asked me to return the next day with my Bible; I did, and we began studying the scriptures together. This was my first experience of a one-on-one Bible study. We talked about the power of the Holy Spirit and the lives of the Apostles who lived with the Spirit's power. I was reminded that I received these gifts in the sacrament of Confirmation earlier in my life, and now I needed to release the power to work through me.

This was a real game-changer for me, and I decided then and there that I would begin the race and I wouldn't turn back. I asked the Holy Spirit to come and be released through me so that I may live in *victory and power*. I accepted the teaching as true, I claimed it for myself, and I gave up my own control; I *let go and let God*. I began a journey to spiritual wellness and becoming blessable. I read from my Bible every day before I left the house or hotel. I offered my day and my work to glorify God, and I watched and prayed for four years as he infused my life with blessings, growing my businesses and enriching my life.

I began to mature in matters of faith and understanding. Wisdom was given to me about matters I truly hadn't yet understood. Today, the spiritual facet is of prime importance for me on the list of E5.

But my transformation wasn't instant, of course; it required real effort and an unwavering faith on my part. I dedicated my successes to Christ by doing what was required of me, tithing properly. I learned to give of my time, energy, talent, and treasure to the good of God's church and charitable organizations. I have taught this principal with amazing results. People who tithe properly with proper motive and spirit become blessable 100% of the time.

Blessability brings about peace. When you live with awareness of God's presence with you at all times, and you submit your life to him in all things, you become blessable. The effort you put into the practice of these principles becomes an honor, never a burden, because living this life of E5 frees you from the chains of doubt, loneliness, anxiety, and the feeling of hopelessness. Instead you *trust* in his great plans for you, you live with the *awareness* of his loving presence, your life unravels itself and becomes graciously *controllable* through God's blessings, and you have great *hope* in his goodness and mercy that has been bestowed to you because of your fidelity to his great plans!

When I first met Mark, he told me directly that the spiritual aspect of my life was the strongest of the five. I've always had, from the time I was a young boy, a strong sense of my faith; it's always been a priority in my life to have a relationship with God. This priority is what drove me to receive my undergraduate degree in Theology. This "head-relationship" with God reinforced my "heart-relationship" with God. Mark made me aware, however, that the lack of balance in the other four areas of my life was throwing off my spiritual wellbeing. For example, with my lack of order in finances, I found I was not tithing properly. Or, with the lack of importance put on my physical wellbeing, I was putting sleep before prayer in my list of priorities.

Mark also gave me a good sense of self-love: *God doesn't make junk!,* he would tell me. Being a Sanguine – Phlegmatic personality, I would often get walked on by others, humiliated, and years of allowing myself to be pushed around in small ways affected my confidence and self-esteem. I was consequently not experiencing God's true love for me, because I didn't believe in it. True spiritual balance consisted of transforming my thought process regarding my worth and my abilities. When I learned to believe in myself, I no longer put limits on God's transforming powers to change my life and bless me as he pleased.

Living with conviction, purpose, passion, and dreams makes you much more reliable on God, because you are doing things that are beyond you, things that you never dreamed you could do. I say to God in my prayer, *I could never do this without you! You are my source of strength, and without you I have nothing, I am nothing!* What a humbling thought, and what a realization that we are totally reliant on his love!

PERSONAL ASSESSMENT: QUESTIONS & APPLICATIONS

Do I believe that I am spiritually balanced? Why or why not?

_____

_____

_____

_____

If I do not feel that I am spiritually balanced, how can I reach balance in my spiritual life?

_____

_____

_____

_____

If I feel that I am spiritually balanced, is there any room for improvement?

_____

_____

_____

_____

What steps am I willing to make to improve my spiritual balance?

_____

_____

_____

_____

Do I trust God and his plans for my life? Why or why not? What can I do to increase my trust in him?

_____

_____

_____

_____

CHAPTER 8

Emotional Balance

When dealing with people, remember you are not dealing with creatures of logic, but creatures of emotion.

~Dale Carnegie

All emotions are pure which gather you and lift you up; that emotion is impure which seizes only one side of your being and so distorts you.

~Rainer Maria Rilke

It is not because the truth is too difficult to see that we make mistakes... we make mistakes because the easiest and most comfortable course for us is to seek insight where it accords with our emotions – especially selfish ones.

~Alexander Solzhenitsyn

It was 2010. The weather was unbeatable at Augusta, Georgia. As the sun shone down on the pristine greens, Phil Michelson was carrying one heavy load. Not only was he walking towards the 18th hole in contention to win the Masters Green Jacket, knowing that his ability to control his nerves could make or break his victory, but he also carried the emotional burden of his wife's and mother's battles with cancer. Amy was watching him from a restful place away from the crowds, and Phil knew what he had to do.

His triumph was an emotional barrage of hugs and tears. Not only for Phil and Amy, but for the crowd around them, and all the spectators watching from their televisions. Phil had won the battle on the greens for his family, for his wife. His battle, for her battle—his triumph, for her triumph.

Phil Mickelson's ability to prioritize and channel the emotions of his personal life in order to accomplish his task and reach his goal was an accomplishment that few could ignore. He was able to use the negative situation of his wife's and mother's battles with cancer and channel the emotions involved into a confidence and drive that won him the Masters.

What is Emotional Balance?

The ability to control your emotive thoughts and reactions to people, internal feelings, and external stimuli with virtue, strength of character, and a clear objective at all times is the path to emotional balance. Emotions can either tear you down or pull you up. They can either create havoc or establish peace. Emotions can either crumble your life or be the vehicle that drives you to your goal.

The choice belongs to the beholder: *you* choose to control your emotions and win, or let them control you, and lose. You have the ability to control your thoughts, to grab hold of your thinking. Not in any circumstance are you made a prisoner of your emotions.

Striving for emotional balance means that you are striving to take hold of those certain situations in life that affect your state of mind and the way you express yourself. The goal is to *get steady and stay steady* with your emotional ups and downs. It is said that you can tell the quality of a person by the size of the things that upset them. You have heard the saying, "don't sweat the small stuff," and in this world, it is mostly small stuff that happens to us on a daily basis. So, train yourself to choose your words wisely, because *what you speak is what you think, what you think is what you believe, and your belief always controls your actions.* You can control emotions with proper thoughts and spoken words.

Recognizing Emotions & Feelings: Good from Bad

You must have the ability to label your state of feeling, identifying the emotions that will get in the way of your achievement of balance. This takes introspection. Turn the radio off. Invite silence into some moments of your life. Consciously look inward, identifying those things that control your days, and how you consistently react to stimuli on a regular basis. Here are some questions you can ask yourself when evaluating your daily habitual actions and reactions based on emotions:

- How do you react to God or the thought of his power in your life?

- How do you react to others and their individual comments, expressions, gestures, actions, or lack thereof?

- How do you react to negative situations such as a traffic jam, losing your keys, or a broken-down computer?

- How do you react to limitations, such as lack of talent, education, love, or frustrations with your career, job status, or financial status?

- How do you react to your own physical burdens such as fatigue and hunger, ailments, or differences?

What are "Out of Control" Emotions?

During World War I the agonizing time spent in the trenches waiting to go over the top into the battlefield was often more debilitating for the soldiers than the actual battle. The anticipation of what was to come created such a paralyzing fear that the emotional, mental, and physical effect was given a name: *No Man's Land Syndrome.* No man wanted to set foot into the land between enemy trenches.

These men lost all control of their faculties because of the overwhelming fear that gripped their entire beings. Nonetheless, men did in fact go over the top. They overcame their fears, despite nerve gas, barbed wire, machine gun fire, mortar fire, and corpses, for their belief in freedom, country, and duty.

The human person can rise above all adversity, even the greatest of all fear, anxiety, and worry. *Never doubt your abilities and your strength.* Never doubt that you can overcome any emotional adversity that may seem to have a grip on your entire being.

Why do I Need Emotional Balance?
(What's in it for me?)

When I was 26 years old and into my third year of youth ministry, I was un-mentored and knew little about true leadership. My wife was pregnant with our 3rd child and I naturally felt the demands of our growing family. The youth ministry program that I was developing was becoming more and more demanding in its need for growth. I had absolutely no inkling as to where my life was heading career-wise, no vision for the future, and no idea what steps to take in order to solidify a stable future for my family. We had a glaringly-problematic money shortage because I simply did not have an adequate salary. My home management responsibilities were neglected and slowly building into an unmanageable list of to-dos. My two children had unpreventable and un-delayable health complications, medical bills were adding up, and the upcoming labor and delivery only increased the stream of healthcare payments. I was losing a grip on my life. The pressure I felt to leave my ministry and to find a better-paying job was mounting, and the stress and emotional disillusionment that resulted landed me in the hospital with the effects of a heart condition.

An entirely stress-free lifestyle is virtually impossible in this fast-paced, demanding world. With financial burdens, health worries, family demands, career quandaries, and so many more elements that can throw our equilibrium off, emotional balance is a necessity if you are to keep it all together. Luckily, I learned this lesson just in the nick of time.

How do I Apply Emotional Balance?

Self-Knowledge: Temperament & Love Language

Each temperament has a particular way to deal with emotions and emotional distress. I will briefly review the temperaments and outline the typical emotive responses belonging to each. Again, I stress that a deeper understanding of your temperament is pivotal to your self-realization and growth, and can be achieved by reading Art and Larraine Bennett's book *The Temperament God Gave You.*

1. **Choleric**

This temperament exudes confidence and an aura of leadership. When a Choleric walks into a room, everyone notices him. Cholerics are fighters and enjoy the battle. Sometimes they look for the fight. They are extreme "Type A" personality and loyal to the death, a protector of the underdog, and an excellent partner in a business. Emotionally, the Choleric charges ahead with passion and intensity, and feels words very deeply. Occasionally the impact of harsh words causes him to be easily hurt, at which point he will plan revenge or completely write off the other person. On the other hand, the Choleric emotionalizes trust and loyalty and returns the same with enduring friendship.

2. **Sanguine**

This temperament is the life of the party. A Sanguine has excellent skills for making people feel at ease. They are lovable and funny, and almost always carefree. A Sanguine can be forgetful and not detail-oriented. They are the ones to cheer you up if you are down. They can light up a room with laughter upon arrival. Emotionally, the Sanguine backs off when confronted with controlling people or too many details for them to address. This emotional shut-down can lead to temporary depression. However, the Sanguine sees joy and laughter in almost every situation which is how they overcome depression; this action may cause a disconnection from reality. Sanguines are perplexed by mean people, a real turn-off for them. Overall, the ups and downs of a Sanguine are mostly emotionally-driven.

3. Phlegmatic

Phlegmatic personalities are the ones who make great leaders because they gather information calmly and succinctly, then make well thought-out decisions. They can be misunderstood as aloof or snobby because they tend to be quiet and unresponsive at times, especially in a new group setting. A Phlegmatic would rather listen than talk. They prefer little attention in groups. They need peace at all costs; confrontation is to be avoided. You will know the Phlegmatic as the "wall flower" sitting quietly in the corner, pleasant but rather unconcerned about the rest of the room. Unless engaged directly, a Phlegmatic will rarely start the conversation. Emotionally, the Phlegmatic is the calmest of all temperaments during stressful times and overall remains consistently stable in his emotional swings. In addition, the Phlegmatic tends to not show emotion or reactions too quickly. He is moderate, not intense, and content with everyday, but never complacent. A Phlegmatic internalizes and ponders, allowing him to be quick to listen and slow to speak, which makes for a great friendship._

4. Melancholic

This temperament is the most detailed of all. Melancholics thrive on order and see to it that those in their care are in order. They make great accountants and controllers of data and are very responsible. They will find themselves engaging others, especially new people, in a controlled group setting. Socially, they are uncomfortable talking about themselves, and will ask a series of questions about you to avoid personal questions about themselves. Melancholics have a need to know things and people so that they can categorize them for future reference. Personally, I love the Melancholic personality in the workplace; no one seems to finish a task better! They are sometimes fearful, based upon a thought or a maybe-this-will-happen attitude. Melancholics tend to be the glass-half-empty type. Emotionally, Melancholics may find it difficult to relax until all the details of the day are done and the list for tomorrow is written. They tend to have competitive and active emotions when they are challenged.

Take some time to go through these questions and answer them as honestly as you can:

- What have you determined your temperament to be?

- Do you think that you react with your emotions or your logic?

- In what area of your life do you find it hardest to channel your emotions into something positive?

Managing your Emotions (for Yourself & Others)

To manage your emotions means to make practical use of the emotions which drive you toward your goals, and to eradicate the emotions which have a negative effect on your balance and goal-oriented state of mind.

1. **Your Attitude is Dictated by your Thoughts**

External application of your emotions can be called your *disposition* or your *attitude. A positive attitude can take you places!* Of course, attitude is not everything: just because your teenage daughter is really positive about driving your car perfectly the first time she gets behind the wheel, chances are, she won't succeed. Success comes with a combination of talent, skill (ability), practice and preparation, and focus. These are the attributes that can be likened to the hands that steer a car. But positive attitude, the external manifestation of positive thinking, is the right foot that drives the vehicle and gives it speed.

What you say is what you think, what you think is what you believe, and your belief controls your actions.

Believe in God. Believe in yourself. Believe that you are God-Powered and that God wants you to be successful (to become all that you can be) and that you have all the tools it takes to reach success. This belief is the stimulus behind your thoughts, your words, and your actions.

My niece is an incredible violinist. She has unbelievable talent, but her talent is not the only factor in her success story. She has put an incredible amount of effort, focus and determination, practice and practice and more practice, into perfecting her skill. From the age of four, her dedication has been enviable.

I remember the first time I saw her perform on stage as a young adult, when her self-awareness, and the awareness of the presence of others, had peaked. She walked onstage, dressed beautifully, with a hunched shuffle that screamed insecurity. Her awkwardness was obvious and painful, but fleeting, because once she raised her violin to her shoulder and played the first note, she took the audience's breath away.

She always believed in the power of her music, but had to learn to believe in the power of her presence. Her belief pervaded her thought process, and her thoughts controlled her actions. As a young adult, she now walks onstage not only with a beautiful dress, but with a beautiful stature, her head held high. She captures the audience from the first step onto the stage.

2. **Words of Affirmation: a Tool to Managing your Emotions**

We have already visited the ways in which words of affirmation help you to achieve your dreams and goals. What I want to explore with you now is the renewal of your emotional balance that can take place simply through the use of words of affirmation.

We all struggle with bouts of stress and anxiety in varying degrees. It is a normal part of life in this fast-paced world in which we live. Words of affirmation have the power to change one's attitude, which in effect can change the way we face the world. Words of affirmation are like the salt that renews a bland meal into something appealing and enjoyable, or the beautiful sound of one's own name spoken with love.

I was recently on a bus trip to Washington, D.C. with a bus full of teenagers. Anyone who has driven in that city knows that the road system is nothing less than utter confusion. Needless to say, after a late start to begin with, in the first 20 minutes of our 8-hour trip home, the bus driver got us inexorably lost.

Morale was low. One of my parent-volunteers had one negative comment after another, bemoaning the ill-fortune of the group, who would be facing a painfully arduous trip home, complete with bad weather, moody teens, and anxious parents waiting for their kids to make it home.

I overrode every negative comment with three positive comments. *Hey, we just came back from an amazing experience! At least we're not in a ditch! We have more time to sing songs together! We have tons of food in this bus—let's eat!* With the strategies that I learned, I successfully improved the group's morale and got the busload of teens home, tired but happy.

3. **Channeling your Emotions:**
   Turning a Negative into a Positive

Channeling your emotions differs from managing emotions because, instead of working to eradicate negative emotions altogether, you are *transforming negative (useless) emotions which stem from a negative experience into something positive and useful.* When getting rid of troubling emotions is not an option, you turn them into something advantageous and functional.

Inspiring examples of channeling one's negative emotions into something positive are in the stories behind all the mothers who make up the MADD (Mothers Against Drunk Driving) force. These mothers were able to channel their pain and anger into advocacy. Instead of allowing their lives to drown in the sorrow of the drunk driving situation that changed their lives, they channeled their emotions in order to increase awareness and help others to speak up against drunk driving.

The 2010 incident of the trapped Chilean Miners made headlines worldwide. All 33 men were found alive 2300 feet below ground 17 days after the cave-in, and were finally able to be brought to the surface 69 days after the cave-in.

Those 17 days were critical to their survival. They lived with little hope of ever being found, knowing that their odds were pretty grim. Immediately, there arose two leaders in the group, who helped the rest of the men through the 69 days of entrapment. Mario Gómez, the oldest of the miners, emerged as the spiritual guide, turning a section of their subterranean prison into a chapel, and eventually cooperating with psychologists above ground to keep the other men emotionally sound. Luis Urzúa, the 54-year old shift leader of the group, quickly took the reigns as the group's organizer, demanding structure and routine to apply a sense of normalcy to their days. He instructed the men to all eat together, waiting until all rations were passed through the borehole, to insure their sense of community and brotherhood. Knowing that the elevated emotions of the men could easily run awry, causing dissention and chaos, Luis and Mario quickly collected their own negative emotions and channeled them into a role of organized, positive leadership. They played a critical part in saving the lives of all 33 men.

Benefits of Emotional Balance

Positive thinking, good judgment and reason, and a joyful and positive outlook are sure qualities of a person who is emotionally balanced. Just as the two miners and the blind leper, you will be able to rise to the top, just as cream always rises to the top, into a leadership role that attracts others to you. Balance is recognizable to others: they recognize it as harmony. Emotional balance will give you the edge that you need, regardless of your temperament.

Harmony, or balance, coupled with good judgment and reasons are powerful and complementary.

Personal Experience of Emotional Balance

Mark's Experience:

My path to emotional balance came about in small steps and continues to this day through a process of consistent study and reflection of the two books, *The Temperament God Gave You* and *The 5 Love Languages*. Once I discovered my hard-wired emotional and love languages, my questions about my behavior were answered. I knew that I was not always sincere and honest. I played the game to get what I wanted, to win favor and approvals. Sometimes my behavior was not pretty, especially when I was in pursuit during battle.

When I began to understand that this attitude derived from my natural Choleric tendency to need to win battles, as well as my natural desire to be affirmed deriving from my primary love language, I could begin awareness of my actions as they related to others. One of the great tragedies of our day is the "all about Self" generation. Because of this self-centered mentality, a wall has been built between the Self and the Other, disabling them from developing intimate spiritual and emotional relationships.

Once I could put a filter and a throttle on the emotional hard-wiring, a new characteristic appeared in me: humility. One distinct benefit was that my marriage improved dramatically with my ability to humble and discipline my selfish needs and wants in favor of the needs of the Other. Through the process of E5, my relationships with my children and others improved dramatically. I changed the way I approached life, from what *I* want, what *I* think, and what *I* feel, to what *God* wanted for me, which was to be selfless for the good of others, which is a true relationship and ex-change of love. It was only then that I began to receive "the peace of God that surpasses all understanding…" as talked about in Philippians 4:7.

I tend to be very sensitive to the words and actions of others (a very Sanguine trait, and also particular to those whose primary love language is Words of Affirmation). I would have a difficult time coping with my emotions when relationships went wrong: with my wife, my children, my friends, or my co-workers. I would even imagine words or actions to mean more than they did, or to mean something differently than they did. I had *vain imagina-tion*: I would have imaginary scenarios play in my head that would cause me anxiety, imagining that others were angry with me be-cause of something that I said or did, or reading into a look that I received from a person that could have meant nothing at all. This vain imagination took away from my productivity towards my goals, because I would be worrying and fretting instead of staying level headed and accomplished at things that actually mattered. When I learned about temperaments and proper emotional bal-ance, I was able to even myself out; I could understand why people acted the way they did because of the fundamentals of who they were, and I learned not to take things so personally. An affirma-tion that especially helped me keep emotionally balanced during the day-to-day ins and outs was simple but clear: *If it doesn't affect me in a positive way in the next two to five years, don't think about it or don't do it.* I wouldn't let negative or worrisome thoughts fester.

I also learned that I needed to protect myself from certain emo-tionally-distressing situations. In my marriage, for example, I knew that money could be a source of emotional strain. I was able to use my financial balance to become more emotionally stable. I also became aware of the good habits that I could implement in order to keep my wife and children happier at home: for example, giving each person special one-on-one time every week, or making sure I was part of the bedtime routine of stories and prayers, tuck-in and kisses when I was home.

A book worthy of mention is Gary Smalley's book *If He Only Knew: What No Woman Can Resist.* Smalley raised greater awareness in my emotions and attitudes that affect my family life, and steer away from potential emotional imbalances due to disagreements or frustrations in my marriage.

PERSONAL ASSESSMENT: QUESTIONS & APPLICATIONS

Do I believe that I am emotionally balanced? If not, where can I apply more balance emotionally?

At home with spouse, children:

_____

_____

_____

_____

With extended family such as parents, siblings:

_____

_____

_____

_____

In the workplace with boss, employees, co-workers:

_____

_____

_____

_____

In social circumstances:

_____

_____

_____

_____

With external influences, distractions, frustrations:

_____

_____

_____

_____

CHAPTER 9

Mental Balance
Changing your Culture
of Thought

*Happiness doesn't depend on any external conditions,
it is governed by our mental attitude.*

~Dale Carnegie

We are what we believe we are.

~C.S. Lewis

It was September 11th, 2001.

The city of New York was in a crisis it had never experienced. As the Twin Towers collapsed and took thousands of people with them, the rest of the nation and the world stood motionless, stunned, watching the television screens and listening to the radio transmitting the horrors of the scene in Manhattan. Amidst all the death, fear, and pain, one thing was clear to one man alone: he had to be the epitome of strength and reason amidst the disaster. He had to convince his crumbling city to resist defeat. This was a tall order, for even he felt the temptation to break down and cry. He didn't: he led the search for victims, the city clean-up and rejuvenation projects, and allowed his people to mourn while rejecting fear and renewing hope. He thanked the heroes and made sure their stories were immortalized through the 9-11 museum project. He kept his composure, because he was the parent who doted on his lost and suffering children.

In reminiscing of the 9-11 trials, Mayor Giuliani admitted, "When I said the city would be stronger, I didn't know that. I just hoped it. There are parts of you that say, 'Maybe we're not going to get through this.' You don't listen to them." This is the sign of a man who has strong mental capacities, who is able to step up to his leadership role regardless of his initial inclination to cower. Throughout his years of leadership, he trained himself to properly react to the situation at hand, even if it was one of the biggest catastrophes to date on American soil.

What is Mental Balance?

Mental balance is to be equipped to properly process and react to all demands and experiences in a way that will help you achieve your dreams and goals, without breaking any of man's laws or God's laws. Mental balance is the ability to process all of life's demands in an orderly, stable manner. When a situation comes at us, we react. We must have the ability to properly process the reality we live in.

WE HAVE AN APP FOR THAT

In today's world of Smart Phones and super-smart computers, there is an application, or "app," for almost anything you can think of, from translating your message to any imaginable language, to learning which constellations you are looking at simply by holding up your computer to the sky. Let's apply this world of apps to our mental reality: what if we were equipped with an app that could tell us exactly how to deal with every demand of everyday life? Without this kind of app, we would be less efficient, we would learn the "hard way" by stumbling through difficult situations. What if I told you that in achieving mental balance, you would be adding that very app to your internal hard drive? This is essentially what we do when we create good habits and stick to them. We create a mental app that guides us towards our dreams and goals.

What are some mental apps?

- Your attitude: how to think positively

- Control of your emotions: how to relate to others (your spouse, children, friends, etc.)

- Knowing your strengths

- Knowing your temperament and the temperament of others

Mental balance does not require genius. Our IQ does not dictate our level of ability in the realm of mental balance. It is the combination of *humility, discipline, purposefulness, and proper Vertical Alignment* that are the makeup of mental balance.

1. Humility

Living within the acceptance and reality of your limitations gives you the capacity to determine your reactions to experiences. In other words, humility helps you to have an objective view of where in your character you need to grow. Many years ago when I first began meeting with my mentor, one of the first things he asked me was if my finances were in order. He asked me pointed questions such as what amount was in my checking account and what I spent every month. He could see by my vague response and look on my face that I had no idea. It took great humility on my part to own up to my misunderstanding of my personal responsibility. But with this humility, I was able to recognize this weakness and take control of an area in my life that I had previously left in disorder. Without humility and recognition of my weaknesses, I could not have grown in responsibility and balance in this area of my life.

2. Discipline

We must all suffer from one of two pains: the pain of discipline or the pain of regret. The difference is discipline weighs ounces while regret weighs tons.
~Jim Rohn

To keep the lamp burning we have to keep putting oil in it.
~Mother Teresa of Calcutta

Once you learn to quit, it becomes a habit.

~Vince Lombardi

Discipline is a key component to mental balance. God has given us the wonderful gift of our intellect and it is up to us how we use it. Only in building positive habits through discipline can we begin to grow in character. Only through discipline can we overcome emotions that can hold us back from our personal growth and goals. It takes mental discipline, for example, to wake up at 6 o'clock when it is a cold, dark winter morning. You have a choice to make when your alarm sounds: follow your emotional repulsion for the discomfort of getting up, shut off the alarm, and curl up under your covers; or, use your discipline, listen to your conscience, and get up, start your morning reflection, look over your 10-10-10, prepare your schedule for the day, head to the gym... all before your coffee and breakfast with the family.

Which choice builds character? Which choice leads us to achieve balance? Which choice will prepare you to win?

All throughout the day these types of situations come about. All through the day you make choices, and discipline allows you to make the most virtuous choices that put you ahead of the crowd. Let us keep in mind Jim Rohn's advice: "We must all suffer from one of two pains: the pain of discipline or the pain of regret. The difference is discipline weighs ounces while regret weighs tons."

3. **Purposefulness**

Hope, vision, a dream, anticipation, foresight... these are all synonyms that give you the drive to live with determination, drive, virtue, and discipline. If you live a life of purpose, with a vision of your goals and dreams for the future, this drives you forward with mental agility. With purposefulness, every step you take is taken with determination.

Why do I Need Mental Balance? (What's in it for Me?)

YOUR ATTITUDE IS A PRODUCT OF YOUR THOUGHTS

If you foster negative thoughts on a regular basis, this will show through your attitude. If you choose to wear gray-colored glasses, you will see the world perpetually in gray. Your attitude controls the outlook and flow of your life and the efficiency and effectiveness to which you will reach your goals.

Being positive is a difference maker! It saves marriages, creates career opportunities, and can even save lives. Do not underestimate the power of your positive attitude, for your own good and for the good of others around you. It is said that negativity spreads more quickly than positivity. Where will negativity take you with your friends, your career, your family? Make your positive attitude attractive and contagious, and you will notice the transformation within you and around you.

THE 4 PHASES OF KNOWLEDGE

The 4 Phases of knowledge outline the stages we pass through as we learn more about ourselves, others, and the world in which we live. It is a guideline to which we can apply our own growth of understanding.

- **I don't know what I don't know**: you have not yet achieved the level of knowledge that allows you to see outside your box; you simply have no idea how further knowledge could open up your possibilities. You bring with you all your bias and prejudgments from your environment and associations. All the inputs you have received to date are in this tiny phrase, "you know what you know and you don't know what you don't know."

- **I know what I don't know**: you are aware that there is more knowledge to be learned, a way to open up your possibilities, but you just don't know what that knowledge is.

- **I grow and know and it starts to show**: the growth in knowledge starts to change you into a more balanced person with greater possibilities.

- **I simply grow because of what I know**: the knowledge you have obtained has opened you up to countless possibilities

Mental Fitness: Like Physical Fitness

As a single footstep will not make a path on the earth, so a single thought will not make a pathway in the mind. To make a deep physical path, we walk again and again. To make a deep mental path, we must think over and over the kind of thoughts we wish to dominate our lives.

~Henry David Thoreau

Perhaps it is easier to make goals for ourselves physically because the end product is visually apparent. However, those of us who make muscle-toning, fat-trimming goals know that we cannot accomplish our plan with one visit to the gym or one run around the block: it takes methodical, persistent habits in order to see and feel the results. Being physically fit requires creating a plan, exercising that plan, and mental toughness to stick it through.

Our mental capacities are intimately dependent upon the training and "exercise" we offer our minds. We have a responsibility to stay mentally fit in order to stay out of complacency, keeping our mental 'muscles' agile and adept. Complacency is the enemy of mental fitness.

We are the Sum of our Influences

We are born "takers." From a very young age, you become what you see, what you hear, the reactions that you encounter through your parents and your grandparents, the influences from television…. All of these play a part in your development. We all have a selfish, self-sustaining pride that is a part of us. In order to change this ego-centeredness, you must think back into your past to figure out your own ways: why do I have that habit? How do I view responsibility? Why do I treat women that way? The way we act and react today is because of the influences we had yesterday, good or bad.

How to Attain Mental Balance

We all need a Mentor or a guide. Mentorship can be received in different forms such as live contact, or through books or audio material. A Mentor is a trusted advisor who helps teach, train, educate, and motivate you to be who you are meant to be. It is ultimately up to *you* to choose to become the best you can be, or just the easy version of you. A Mentor is someone who can look at your life objectively, help you recognize that you need help, define your areas of non-giftedness, root out bad habits, and create new, good habits that reshape all five pillars of your human reality into proper balance and a sound culture of thought; in other words, achieving E5. Somewhere after our school days, we stop seeking guidance and teaching from others. We self-mentor out of an attitude of independence and a lack of understanding that lifelong learning is pivotal to success. Mentorship is the single most significant event that has changed my life. Once I got my big fat ego out of the way, and humbled myself to listen to another man who had the fruit on his tree that I wanted, everything began to change.

Before I had a Mentor, I would wake up every day with dread. I would worry about my day's schedule, my ability to perform at my job. Once I had a mentor, my paradigm shifted, my focus changed. My life began to show it. I had a positive attitude on life. I believed that God was on my side and that I could attack every obstacle and win. This was an amazing transformation, and it came as the result of knowledge and the Power of the Spoken Word. Remember, words have the power to bring either life or death! I became word-conscious and created habits of speaking what I wanted, not the things I did not want or I feared.

On the reality series *The Biggest Loser*, we are shown the horrors of massive obesity. The tools these people are given throughout the weeks at the ranch working to lose weight and regain their feelings of dignity and worth are invaluable to their physical, emotional, mental, and spiritual health.

CULTURE OF THOUGHT

CT is a perspective. If your CT is good, you don't need to change it. CT is what you have learned and experienced.

You cannot please both God and the world at the same
time. They are utterly opposed to each other in their
thoughts, their desires, and their actions.

~John Vianney

A proper Culture of Thought is a state of mind that is disci-
plined, joyful, kind, compassionate, moral, and just, and is
willed with honor, integrity, and love. This state of mind is
formed by good values, positive associations, and a helpful (not
distracting) environment that will support you to achieve your
dreams and goals. In other words, a sound culture of thought is
needed for your properly formed conscience, which in turn can
receive the word of God through scripture and prayer.

Think virtuously, think responsibly, think maturely, think affir-
matively, think in terms of cause and effect, think in terms of consequences, think in terms of Vertical Alignment, think in terms
of the Golden Rule (do unto others as you would have them do
unto you), and you develop habits that develop your character
into something that is good and pleasing to God.

Some Experiences that Properly Form your Culture of Thought:

- Good mentoring

- Positive associations

- Great books (including scripture)

- Good (wholesome) music

- Other Wholesome Media (television, magazines, etc.)

- Whatever sharpens and builds your 10-10-10 and lifts up

your spirit with positive life-giving seeds that will bring you closer to your dreams and goals

Make choices that protect your Culture of Thought. Treat your mind as a highly-volatile child that latches on to anything it encounters. Keep your mind safe from the junk that clutters so many minds and hearts today. You can do this by asking yourself as you face your daily choices: *Does this break Man's law or God's law?* If so, don't do it!

For the sake of simplicity, let's explore the world of Star Wars. There were two Cultures of Thought: the way of the Jedi and the Dark Side. One culture of thought was revolved around the Good and the Moral; the other culture of thought was immersed in evil, betrayal, and selfishness. Anakin started associating himself with the Emperor, who had an unsound culture of thinking. This tainted his thoughts and he was slowly seduced to the Dark Side. We all know the ending: Anakin becomes Darth Vader. Why does this happen? He begins to pick up certain negative thoughts from the Emperor. Thoughts become negative attitude. Anakin's demise was that he was thinking of his own selfish wants and needs. This is the root of all evil: pride and vanity. In the spirit of Vertical Alignment, putting yourself last is the way to real success (not the type of "success" Darth Vader came to suffer).

A sound culture of thought is going to lead you to *God,* it's going to lead you to developing a long-lasting, fruitful relationship with your spouse, a great relationship with your children, it will make you a man for others.

TRAINING OPTIONS: PROTECTING YOUR MIND

Use self-control and wisdom to make the right choices that

protect your mind from garbage. It is important to protect what goes into your mind and your soul, because we are molded from our experiences. Negative people, horror movies, mindless television.... If you need to work on your mind, you need to know what it doesn't need in order to give it what it does need. If you just spent an hour working out, would you leave the gym and eat a bunch of doughnuts? Would you allow that as part of your lifestyle? If you did, it would become counterproductive. Our minds can become scarred by negative influences, and it doesn't forget these negative influences. It is easier to protect yourself altogether than to try to reverse the effects of a negative experience. Protect your mind from harmful inputs.

Mark's Thoughts:

Below is an excerpt from a lesson I wrote on how to minimize the inputs that become distractions in your life or occupy too much space in your mind. This article not only applies to CEOs but to each of us, no matter our position in life.

How to Gain Sleep and Attain Mental Peace

During my 23 years as a business coach I have coached CEOs from a variety of industries, from small start-ups to midsize corporations with $400 Million in revenue and hundreds of employees. One of the common denominators found during the evaluation period of the CEO is a lack of a good night's sleep. I help executives map out the processes of their day to identify the sources and inputs that may be causing their minds to stay on track instead of shutting down at inopportune times for the good night sleep they need. Overwhelmingly, the processes of their days seem to share some commonality that contributes to this challenge. Whether it is excitement, worry, anxiety or just plain exhaustion that keeps an executive from resting, the remedy is foolproof.

Executives of today have five to ten times more sources of input than their CEO counterparts of 30 years ago. Today's executives have instant, up-to-the-minute news online as well as business information being conveyed inter-office more quickly and in more abundance than ever before. They have mobile devices with more power than the best home computer of 20 years ago. They are expected to receive, digest, and act upon voice mail, email, text messaging, calendar prompts, phone alerts, and internet research and data about their businesses, all duplicated on their laptops in their office and at home, bombarding them with information to be absorbed or reacted to. These are seven different daily inputs that executives are expected to respond to and implement! In addition to being deluged with input regarding their business lives, a CEO faces an additional barrage of information on a personal level: the news, entertainment, life's events, world events, stock markets and, of course, the weather, each one from internet, mobile, TV, radio, and print sources. Then, there are sports that executives enjoy either as participants or spectators through various media. More than 36 types of input bring information everyday to busy executives. It is little wonder that today's CEO has trouble sleeping.

The responsibility of a CEO includes the company, the community, their church, their family, and their marriage. These are the responsibilities that the CEO has embraced and managed effectively for decades. But today, with all the other sources of input, the cause of restlessness is simple: the weight of the world, our own world, is thrust upon our shoulders.

"But wait a minute," I point out to my CEO friend, "thrust upon, or chosen?" I remember a time when I had to make that decision, to indulge in all these inputs or to leave some of it behind. I was taught by a very successful entrepreneur, one of my mentors, who had the total package: great business success, great marriage, great health, and great faith life. He even had a great head of hair and looked 20 years younger than he was! He taught me to *control my inputs.* He advised me to only put things into my brain that were necessary, and to remove all non-essential inputs after 7 or 8pm. He said to me, "Why go to bed with the 11 o'clock news on your mind, some natural disaster or some other piece of negative news such as murder, terrorism, or a bad stock market? We can't control it and we may not even need the information. If it doesn't affect our lives in a positive way over the next two to five years, why allow it to fester in our minds?" He told me to *control my inputs, control my thoughts.*

The remedy for interrupted sleep patterns was to remove the weight of the world and as much negativity as possible before going to bed, replacing it with positive inputs. I began to turn off all negative media after 7pm and to read 15-20 minutes from a PMA (positive mental attitude) book before bed. Just those two changes in habit have allowed me to sleep like a happy baby for the past 15 years! Other CEOs who have implemented these two small changes have experienced a 100% success rate with increased sleep and a more peaceful and restful sleep. To this routine, because I am a faith-filled person, I added this prayer: "Thank you, Lord, for a 100% total hedge of protection and peaceful, restful sleep for me and my family."

After about six weeks of this daily routine, I began to feel repulsed by the news and all the negative inputs. I decided to take the advice from my mentor to a higher level, and began implementing a daily routine of controlling inputs all day, not just at nighttime. I gave up all newspaper, radio, and television for a six-month period of time. I began to realize that during the day many of the inputs placed in my mind were useless or harmful. As a result, I began to feel little or no stress and I certainly no longer went to bed with the world's problems on my mind or some weather disaster across the world which would not have an impact on my life over the next 2-5 years of my life. My days began brighter; my ideas and problem-solving skills were sharper, my tolerance greater, and the ability to love my fellow man increased.

Today, people I meet cannot believe I have four children ages 32, 30, 17 & 15 and have been married to my wife for 33 years. I look like my mentor did at my age! Thanks be to GOD I still have my hair and original teeth! I may joke a bit about the solution and the challenges but if, however, you are a CEO who suffers from lack of sleep, then you need to practice this process of controlling your mental inputs. I believe this advice can work for you, too. Give it a try for a week or two. You will gain a restful, peaceful night's sleep. It is life changing!

Vertically-Aligned Thoughts

To reiterate what we've already discussed, Vertical Alignment applies to balance on the mental front because we use our minds to make choices, and proper Vertical Alignment demands decision-making and priority-ordering.

MENTAL TOUGHNESS: ABILITY TO PROPERLY DEAL WITH LIFE'S DEMANDS

Mental toughness does not demand that we become robots, emotionally impenetrable to any given situation. Or, that we become pent-up bottles ready to burst at any moment because we are so preoccupied with putting on a good face. Instead, mental toughness is the ability to smoothly and quickly respond to life's demands in an ethical, reasonable, God-minded way, thus avoiding harmful, wrong thinking.

HABITS

As I have mentioned, it takes 21 days to build a habit. This is a small price to pay for building up a profile of desirable, effective, straight-shooting habits which are essential to effective performance.

Life has a way of controlling us. It has a way of making us follow its patterns. We find ourselves being pulled along on a daily routine that we may or may not enjoy. But *it's what we do to take a hold of each day, hour by hour, that puts us in the game of success.* Do not allow yourself to live on auto-pilot: be in control of the game of life! Wake an hour earlier to get in a morning run, look over your day, forecast potential distractions of the day, read aloud your 10-10-10, equip yourself with the tools you need to make the day successful. Affirm yourself in the mirror as you brush your teeth. Take your hour commute to converse with God or listen to positive-mental-attitude life-building audio material. I could go on with examples, but you get it: take hold of time. Make time more accessible to you; create more time pockets in which you are building your development as an integral human person in simple but meaningful ways. Although not always easy to implement, this is essentially a simple formula for success.

We are in the game of life. The clock is ticking. Do not let life live you. Take a hold of the steering wheel; be an impact player, add depth to your actions, and make every action meaningful moves toward your dreams and goals.

What we are talking about are *habitual actions*. Building habits, one by one, leads to great days. One great day could be the difference maker, leading to months of success. Many great days, back-to-back, in harmony with each other, are the foundational blocks of a fulfilling and meaningful life.

INTELLECTUAL STIMULATION

Taking the term *lifelong learner* to heart is something that we should all do. There is a vast amount of valuable knowledge out there that enriches our spirits and stimulates our intellect. There will never be a time that any one of us can feel that we have learned enough, that there is no more knowledge to be learned that would be valuable to us in any given moment.

Enrich your mind. Believe in its capacities to ever expand and learn. Take on new interests, deepen your knowledge of your faith, your heritage, your country, your history. You will enrich others' lives with your gained knowledge and interesting insights.

SELF-KNOWLEDGE & SELF-MASTERY: KNOWING YOUR STRENGTHS, TEMPERAMENT & LOVE LANGUAGE

1. Knowing Your Strengths Builds Confidence

In their book *Now Discover Your Strengths*, Marcus Buckingham and Donald Clifton describe *strength* as "consistent near-perfect performance in an activity."[17] You are born with certain strengths that are hard-wired, and from this pool of strengths you are given, talents emerge. Mark and I share an interest and talent in golf. But we have different strengths that lend to our talents. Mark's strength is thinking *strategically*, which helps him play a great golf game: he measures the wind, looks at the slope of the green, studies the layout of the course, takes note of the temperature, and so on. My strength is *positivity*, which gives me the right attitude to get the ball in the hole: I believe that, with all the given factors on that given day, I can get the job done, and done well. Our strengths lend differently to our interests and talents.

Knowing your strengths gives you confidence and insight into how you can use those strengths. This knowledge opens you up to the possibilities of making a difference on levels you didn't think possible. Furthermore, with knowledge of your strengths comes knowledge of your non-gifted areas, which, when aware of them, you can begin to channel time away from them and spend more time on using your strengths. If you are able to perceive these time-stealers or blind spots before they occur, you can eliminate them altogether. Practice focusing on your strengths. For example, I have learned that I waste more time making charts and graphs than necessary, so I just don't waste time on them anymore;

I delegate that task. The delegation of my non-gifted areas, namely the minutia of details, frees me up to do what I do best: creative thinking.

Buckingham and Clifton list 34 strengths from which each of us have a top five. I will list these strengths, but in order to understand each one, it would be helpful to read their book.[18]

Achiever	Developer	Learner
Activator	Discipline	Maximize
Adaptability	Empathy	Positivity
Analytical	Fairness	Relator
Arranger	Focus	Responsibility
Belief	Futuristic	Restorative
Command	Harmony	Self-assurance
Communication	Ideation	Significance
Competition	Inclusiveness	Strategic
Connectedness	Individualization	Woo
Context	Input	
Deliberative	Intellection	

To highlight some of these listed strengths, I will share with you my top five.

Belief: *Value-driven, family-oriented, spiritual, ethical, principle-centered, priority-driven.* Belief gives me the foundation to continue on in my ministry. Through my belief system, Vertical Alignment came easily to me, because I hold a high importance on my marriage and family, and I never let my job get in the way of these things. The typical Youth Director burns out in 18 months, but I was able to withstand this statistic. My strength in my belief also helped me in my mentor-student relationship with Mark: I showed him that I was trustworthy, principle-centered, and driven by these values that he shared with me. I have a desire to be a man for others; I want to fill my life up with treasures that I can share with others.

Activator: *Impatient for action, impulsive, quick action on decisions, don't want to be slowed down or micro-managed, know you'll get judged by what you have done.* I didn't realize this was a strength of mine until I was told. I am now completely convinced in this strength of mine. It has given me the ability to really move my ministry forward, to make things happen, create events, increase production. It was also a big player in my movement towards writing this book and making changes in my life for the future. I'm a "let's do it" guy, but I have to be careful not to move too fast, so I can make sure that I am making the right decisions and not moving forward too impulsively, without right judgment. Through this strength, I have learned to align myself with other people who complement my strength with their own (such as Strategic or Deliberative).

Positivity: *Enthusiastic, easily excitable, like fun, light-hearted, glass-half-full mentality, give praise.* As a Sanguine, this strength goes hand-in-hand. When working with people in ministry, there are always down-times, when you or your work is criticized. I have been able to move forward through this by keeping a positive attitude. Being aware of this as my strength has helped me to be the shoulder for others to lean on and the one to help pick them up in times of distress. The danger with this strength is to give false praise or affirmation that covers up real problems, and so I have learned to make sure I am being honest in my positivity.

Responsibility: *Follow-through attitude, trustworthy, dependable, emotionally tied to promises you give, eager to volunteer, inclination to do things right.* I feel that I have a great responsibility to be *more* for others. This drives me to be a better person and to do more for the ministry and for my family.

Futuristic: *Visionary, inspired by what tomorrow could be, hopeful, energize and inspire people toward a good outcome.* I began my marriage off as a poor student while Meredith pulled us through our first year as an Advertising Representative for the local newspaper in our little town. We scraped by that first year, expecting our first child, knowing that big changes and big responsibilities lay ahead. Despite the fact that, after graduation, my wife would be home with our baby and I had no job lined up, I was hopeful in our prospects and inspired by what our future would hold. While my wife worried and fretted, I chose to hold on to this hope even when my first job in ministry was a call to sacrifice for us. My continued vision for the future has greatly influenced the decisions we have made and the way we move forward in our life together.

Mark's top five strengths:

Command: *Take charge, share views with others, not afraid of confrontation, share facts and truth, have presence.* I assess and take control of any situation and lead, and am a presence in the room.

Strategic: *Find best way to do things, distinct thinking, see patterns, practical.* I can think and see around corners, am a problem solver, and am good in planning and risk management.

Activator: *Impatient for action, impulsive, quick action on decisions, don't want to be slowed down or micro-managed, know you'll get judged by what you have done.* I have a built-in sense of urgency, do-it-now don't-delay get-started attitude, and I energize others into action.

Belief: *Value-driven, family-oriented, spiritual, ethical, principle-centered, priority-driven.* I believe in people more than they believe in themselves, and I see the good first.

Significance: *Want to be recognized, heard, appreciated, want to stand out, have an independent spirit, want work to be a way of life not a job, a teacher.* I see how everything has importance no matter how small. Even in volunteer work I only do for the charity what I alone can do that is in my strength zone. I stay away from work not related to my strengths in all areas of my life. I am happier about the time I invest when I feel productive and contributing.

2. Knowing Your Temperament Gives You the Edge

In relationships, social situations, business settings, meetings, you understand how you interact with and react to people and circumstances. You have the edge with the knowledge of your temperament which is very important from a mental standpoint. Also, you are able to perceive how others perceive you with the knowledge of temperaments. For example, I am a phlegmatic and I tend towards passivity. But there are times when I need to be bold. I can rise up from the restraints of my temperament and use the positive qualities of other temperament to reach my goal and accomplish my task. As a manager at work, for example, with the knowledge of others' temperaments, you are able to orchestrate and accommodate their certain temperaments to make them feel comfortable on the team and help them perform to their greatest potential.

3. Knowing Your Love Language Builds Empathy

Love language is the key to showing people that you genuinely care. Everyone wants to feel loved and appreciated, and that who they are and what they do matters. Knowing how different people in your family, organization, or church community, feel their own yearnings for love, can better enable you to help them feel loved and appreciated. In turn, you will be more appreciated by others because they will see that you understand and genuinely care about them. Empathy is a gift.

Benefits of Mental Balance

Here is a quick go-to list underlying some major benefits to a life of mental balance:

- Application of knowledge that equips you for success in character-building, relationship-building, goal-reaching

- Development of mental toughness to handle internal and external stimuli (inputs) with prudence

- Positive outlook on life which opens up opportunities and results in the fulfillment of your dreams and goals

- Development of a sound culture of thinking which moves you closer to your dreams and goals

- Development of mental discipline which commits you to reaching your dreams and goals

Personal Experience of Mental Balance

Mark's Experience:

When mentoring a man in his late thirties who ran a company with multiple subsidiaries, we discussed the next phase of his development in the growth plan for his company. He wanted to invest money and expand into uncharted territory to serve a need that seemed to be unfulfilled in his industry. His idea had merit and the void to be filled was real. He could have served others. However, his approach wasn't the best and when he prayed for guidance he felt strongly moved that he should proceed despite caution from me and others on his board. The plan was launched with great excitement and enthusiasm and almost immediately flopped to failure. He was dejected and confused why God would not have blessed this endeavor after all he prayed about it. He was ready to quit altogether. I explained to him that God answers all prayer and that even NO was an answer. I explained further that sometimes no is for our own good. I asked him to take more time to consider other options and ways he could more effectively launch the program. Within 6 months he had met more people and shared his vision with others who then joined his team, brought a fresh perspective. Together, they relaunched the program. This time reaching out to a national customer who agreed that the launch would benefit them and the program began to flourish. "In God's timing, delay is not denial". This man had to hang tough and keep on thinking through the plan, eventually his faith and hope delivered a better and even bigger solution than his original idea.

Here is another example of mental toughness concerning marriages and how you speak about your spouse. My wife and I speak to engaged couples in our diocese to help prepare them for marriage. We tell the couples to be very careful and word conscience when out with guys or the girls. When the other ladies start talking about their lazy, good for nothing, snack eating and sports watching machine at home and how he doesn't do as he is told, we tell the engaged couples to get mentally tough and not join in with them because if you do (even if you don't believe it) and are just joining to be a part of the group, it is harmful to the mental picture of your knight in shining armor. Soon, he may start to look a little dull because your thinking allows for a negative picture to develop. Men, don't you dare brag about the old lady at home and that you wear the pants in the family and how you can stay out as late as you want. We know you're lying! As soon as you get home, you'll walk in quietly looking to see if anyone is up and how much trouble you're in. Men, if you speak poorly of your beloved, you'll look at her differently. She will pick up on your vibe and suspect that you have done something you shouldn't have. Be respectful to others especially your spouse. Refuse to gossip or create negative mental pictures in your mind. Choose a life of joy with your future spouse. One last closing thought: ladies, when you do get home and he is asleep on the couch with remote in one hand and a bowl of popcorn in the other with ESPN blaring, remember to say "bless his heart he was so tired he fell asleep waiting up for me to get home". Mental toughness is needed in all aspects of life. It is how to keep positive mental pictures that turn into thoughts.

Before I began my E5 journey, I never put much emphasis on reading. Outside of the books I needed to read for my education, I had only read a handful of books from cover to cover for my own edification. While a student, I remember having so much to read at once, that I would cut corners to save time by drinking right out of the coffee carafe! A college student has so much reading material to cover, that "me time" would not consist of extracurricular reading! I didn't know how to apply knowledge at that time of life; I hadn't yet learned how to connect the dots. Information was being thrown into the cavern of my brain with no organized system. The concept of being a lifelong learner was simply not part of my vocabulary, because I hadn't discovered my passion for it.

After being introduced to E5 and applying it to my own life, I began to thirst for personal growth in all areas of my life. I began asking interesting, successful CEOs out to lunch with me for a "lunch-'n-learn," during which I would ask them questions about their drive, their dreams, their habits, and their achievements. The wisdom I gathered through my conversations with these men has been invaluable in my own personal growth.

I have fallen in love with the goal of reaching my fullest potential as an individual. Time spent watching television has turned into time devouring great books that help me reach my goals; time spent listening to mindless radio has turned into time listening to life-enriching talks, productive thinking, or praying. I began to understand that the habits I build today make a difference in my tomorrow, that I needed to equip myself *daily* to achieve my dreams and my goals.

Personal Assessment: Questions & Applications

Do I believe that I have a sound Culture of Thought (does it break any of God's laws or man's laws)? If not, what can I do to change my Culture of Thought?

Music:

_____

_____

_____

_____

_____

Television:

_____
_____
_____
_____
_____

Internet and Other Media:

_____
_____
_____
_____

Books and Magazines:

_____
_____
_____
_____

Friends I keep:

_____
_____
_____
_____

Quality of Conversation:

_____

_____

_____

_____

_____

Do I strive to stimulate myself intellectually? If not, how can I better take on the lifestyle of a lifelong learner? (For example, enriching books such as scripture, temperaments, love languages, strength finders; national and international news, learning new helpful tasks, developing my talents, etc.)

_____

_____

_____

_____

_____

Do I properly deal with life's demands on a daily basis with mental agility and toughness? If not, how can I begin to apply mental agility?

At home with spouse, children:

_____

_____

_____

_____

_____

With extended family such as parents, siblings:

_____

_____

_____

_____

_____

In the workplace with boss, employees, co-workers:

_____

_____

_____

_____

_____

In social circumstances:

_____

_____

_____

_____

_____

With external influences, distractions, frustrations:

_____

_____

_____

_____

_____

What phase of knowing do I currently belong? How do I make such a conclusion?

_____

_____

_____

_____

_____

How can I apply my discoveries of my love language and temperament to achieve mental balance?

Love Language:

_____

_____

_____

_____

_____

Temperament:

_____

_____

_____

_____

_____

CHAPTER 10

Physical Balance

Physical fitness is not only one of the most important keys to a healthy body, it is the basis of dynamic and creative intellectual activity.

~John F. Kennedy

Rick Hoyt was born different. The doctors told Mom and Dad to send him and keep him in an institution, because he would amount to nothing but a burden. Instead, they carried him home from the hospital and treated him like any other child. They showered him with love and set him up for achievement. They equipped him with a computer so that he could communicate.

Rick was smart. He had dreams and desires. He completed high school, and then college. He proved himself to be much more than "nothing."

More than anything, Rick had a love for sports. He heard of a local charity run for an injured athlete and asked his dad if they could participate. They ended second to last, running 5 miles together, Rick in a wheel chair while Dad pushed him along. This began a love affair with running: he felt free from his disability as he ran with his father.

Dick and Rick Hoyt became regulars in marathons, triathlons, and Iron Man competitions. They run with each other, with a purpose and a message: you CAN do anything you put your mind to.

Dick Hoyt used his physical capabilities to bring joy, hope, and peace to his son and his home. He found spiritual peace by living out his calling to give his son a sense of freedom from his physical disabilities. He found emotional comfort by making a difference in his son's life and in the lives of others through their message. He found mental balance in his focus and drive. He was able to find balance in all areas of life because of his physical commitment to lend his capable arms and legs so that his son could accomplish his own dreams and goals. In this way, Dick Hoyt found his significance.

What is Physical Balance?

Physical Balance is the awareness of and application of healthy habits for your personal wellness which affects every other facet of life, including your personal relationships.

Why do I Need Physical Balance? (what's in it for me?)

PERSONAL PERFORMANCE IN ALL AREAS OF LIFE: PHYSICAL WELLNESS AFFECTS EVERY OTHER FACET OF LIFE

Physical wellness affects every other facet of life. If you are unwell physically, this may lead to exhaustion and irritability, or may limit your efficiency in other matters of life. The equation is simple. If you eat too many sweets, you may wind up with diabetes. If you lack in vitamin D, you will wind up with a host of problems including immense fatigue. Lack of energy sucks up your time, your will power and your success. I could give more examples, but I think this is straight forward. Personal wellness in relation to healthy food choices, exercise regimens, fidelity to medication and vitamin routines, and regular physical check up are four ways you can control the length of your life and the productivity and happiness levels of your life. It is also important to control your thoughts to focus on good health, and to guard against situations that may put you in harm's way.

Mark's thoughts:

Speaking the desired result into existence with affirmations is a powerful health tool. I say to myself: "I'm going to live to be 100 and still play golf! Thanks be to God I still have all my hair and original teeth! Thank you Lord for the gift of 100% total health spiritually, emotionally, mentally, physically and financially!" Practice claiming the victory and power over your health.

For Those Who Love You & Count on You

Knowing that the length of your life may possibly be in direct relation with the amount of physical fitness and wellbeing you fit into your lifestyle should spur you on to a life of healthy living for the sake of your loved ones. It is selfish to ignore your physical health to the detriment of the quality of your life, especially when you have a spouse, children, or parent counting on your own wellbeing.

Preventative Health

Again, this is simple. Our purpose is to outline these important aspects of your overall health so that you can fit these into your time management and goals. How many of us let dentist appointments slides? How many of us ignore a little heart murmur? How many of us pass off the continuous fatigue we may feel from lunchtime until we crash at night? You need to take a hold of your responsibility to live a healthy life through preventative measures:

- Stay on track with your regularly scheduled doctor visits

- Keep your annual physical exams

- Stay on track with your medications

- Exercise regularly

- Get healthy amounts of sleep

- Stay on a healthy vitamin regimen

- Know your family history

- Learn more about healthy eating habits and make healthier choices

- Learn moderation in food and drink for sustained weight control

This all takes will power. We all have the power to choose "yes" or choose "no." In fact, we make "yes" choices and "no" choices hundreds of times a day. If you become more aware of these choices, you can create an internal checks and balances system that guides you when you are tempted to go the unhealthy route at any given time of the day.

How do I Apply Physical Balance?

SELF-KNOWLEDGE: TEMPERAMENT

Your attitude towards physical discipline is dependent upon your temperament. You may love to feel the burn of a good workout, or you may despise breaking a sweat. Either way, in order to be successful in maintaining a healthy lifestyle and be physically balanced, *you must learn how to work with your temperament.* For example, if you are a choleric who hates to lose battles, set attainable goals for yourself each time you head to the gym. If you are a melancholic who loves perfect detail, create a graph of your achievements and add to it after every workout. If you are a sanguine who is social and fun-loving, do your workout with someone you enjoy to spend time with. If you are a phlegmatic who desires reflection time and peace, pick a physical regimen that gives you that needed time and less of a chaotic atmosphere, such as hiking, rowing, or swimming.

DIETARY RESPONSIBILITY, SLEEP, & EXERCISE

Research suggests that 2 out of 3 Americans are now living overweight or obese. The increasing weight of Americans has been a growing problem for decades. Our national obsession with being skinny or muscular and the various ways to achieve this goal, bogus or not, hasn't seemed to fix the situation. And yet, we are all very well versed in the three components to a healthy body: dietary responsibility, proper sleep, and regular exercise. To add to this list, eliminate all the bad habits (such as smoking, excessive drinking, overeating, etc.) that infringe on your wellness. Evaluate your own tendencies in these three areas and determine where you could develop better habits.

BALANCE IN OTHER AREAS OF LIFE

You may be wondering why you just can't stick with your physical goals. Don't be so quick to assume that it is a problem with the physical balance pillar. You could be struggling with mental toughness that keeps you from following through with your goals. Or perhaps, do you use eating as an emotional bandage? Do you reach for that snack when you're anxious or nervous? Likewise, you could be sorely lacking in time management and waste all your evenings sitting in front of the television after a long day sitting in front of a computer behind a desk, getting no time in for physical activity. My personal experience was that, once I had my spiritual pillar in order, everything else fell into place. Consider which pillar is most pivotal to you, as in, which one helps pull the weight of the rest of the pillars. This may take some thoughtful consideration on your part, but it is well worth it to reach a greater self-awareness in order to understand yourself more deeply.

Benefits of Physical Balance: It Affects the Whole Person!

SPIRITUAL & EMOTIONAL BENEFITS

As I have pointed out, our physical wellbeing affects the whole Person. Your poor self-esteem or lack of energy from poor physical health can weigh down every other aspect of E5. A negative mindset (poor self-esteem) upsets the whole order or E5. Consider this chain of events: You are overweight. Emotionally, you are distraught over it. Spiritually, you cannot even begin to consider that you are worth every blessing God bestows on you because, in your eyes, you are a disappointment. Mentally, you cannot concentrate on your daily tasks and accomplish your goals with success because you are overwhelmed with personal failure. If only you could get a grip on your physical wellbeing, you could put more input and achieve more success in the other areas of E5.

MENTAL BENEFITS: INTELLECTUAL STIMULATION & MENTAL AGILITY

Physical wellbeing is directly linked to intellectual output. In other words, your brain is healthier when your body is healthier, and can perform more efficiently and more effectively than when you are in poor physical health. At work, at home, in volunteer or social setting, you can be more successful, more helpful, more positive, and more agile in your activities.

GENERATIONS

Now I want you to consider this thought: wouldn't it be a shame to develop success habits, become financially successful, attain your dreams and goals, and not enjoy them because you ignored your physical wellbeing? Deteriorating health steals away the fruits of your labor.

You have a responsibility to care for not only yourself in this world, but for your spouse, your children, your parents and greater family, and your community. Your effectiveness as a spouse, parent, child, family member, or community member is compromised if you do not keep your body as at its healthiest capability. The most sobering thought for me is, as I have already mentioned, the time I have in this world: life is already short enough. Do I want to shorten my lifespan by making poor health choices? Don't I owe it to my children and spouse to be around as long as I possibly can?

Be a master of your whole person by becoming the best person you can possibly be in *all* areas. ***This*** is what you were made for!

Personal Experience of Physical Balance

Mark's Experience:

My personal health story was one of neglect until I was 45 years old. I was mostly healthy over the years and I saw a doctor only when absolutely necessary. My youthful years were filled with poor habits such as late nights, drinking, smoking, and eating to excess. My mentor at the time introduced me to the concept that my health was not mine alone, that I was responsible to my wife, children, and others in my employment. He explained that I needed to care about myself enough to do my part in keeping healthy to live a life of prosperity for myself and others.

When I fully understood that others were counting on me and my body, and not just my financial support, I gave up my immature outlook on caring for my health. I began claiming good health and putting forth an effort to visit my family doctor for regular physicals and keeping my subsequent appointments. I went back to the gym for exercise three times a week. I used a skin care system and sunscreen when outdoors. My example of change has been a source of encouragement for others. My wife joined the gym and works out 3-5 days a week. My kids took notice and joined in the exercise program. We eat well, sleep well, and keep stress out of our lives with the use of E5 principals. My energy level is that of a much younger man according to my recent examinations.

As we all age, our bodies change and performance can be effected. Stay on top of it and live well.

The strongest impetus for me to stay healthy is my family. I know that my wife and my children count on me to be strong and healthy, and this drives me. To be completely honest with myself and with you, physical balance hasn't always been my strongest suit. I naturally dislike physical check-ups, I don't like joining other guys in the weight room (give me natural beauty in the woods, instead!), and I would much rather eat a bacon-cheddar cheeseburger than a garden salad! But, as we have reiterated so often in this book, the path to success is not the one most traveled; the path to reaching your fullest potential is not the path of least resistance. And so I use the tools that I have been taught, such as fitting my health regimen to my interests (the outdoors, for instance, or joining Taekwondo with my son as a bonding time) and put my will power into fifth gear with thoughts of reaching my greatest potential as an individual, being a good example for my children, and living side by side my wife until I'm 95!

Personal Assessment: Questions & Applications

How is my physical wellbeing? Ask someone you trust about your physical wellbeing.

_____

_____

_____

_____

_____

Do I feel that I could put more emphasis on my physical health?

_____

_____

_____

_____

_____

If so, how can I rearrange my priorities and/or schedule to fit time in for my health needs? (For example, cooking more healthful meals, going to the gym, etc.)

_____

_____

_____

_____

_____

Do I harbor any bad habits that I could eliminate for my better health? Do I have any health difficulties that stem from my poor judgment? (For example, bad food choices, excessiveness in my eating or drinking, lack of exercise, unmet medicine or vitamin needs, etc.)

_____

_____

_____

_____

_____

CHAPTER 11

Financial Balance

Money isn't the most important thing in life, but it's reasonably close to oxygen on the "gotta have it" scale.

~Zig Ziglar

*Money is power, freedom, a cushion,
the root of all evil, the sum of blessings.*

~Carl Sandburg

Money may be the husk of many things but not the kernel. It brings you food, but not appetite; medicine, but not health; acquaintance, but not friends; servants, but not loyalty; days of joy, but not peace and happiness.

~ Henrik Ibsen

If money is your hope for independence you will never have it. The only real security that a man will have in this world is a reserve of knowledge, experience, and ability.

~Henry Ford

Great-Grandpa Manda lived a humble life as a laborer. He had just married his sweetheart and wanted the best life for her. He had a dream. He also had a problem: the political scene in Hungary was dire and didn't offer much hope.

It was 1913. He bade his family goodbye and, during the secrecy of the night, was smuggled out of the country on a hay carriage. The trip on board the ship was long and arduous, but his dreams kept his spirits high. The Statue of Liberty was the sweetest vision after weeks of sea sickness and anticipation.

From Ellis Island, Ladislaus Manda traveled to West Virginia with one goal in mind: the coal mines. He changed his name to Louis and worked alongside Americans and Immigrants alike for seven years. His frugal lifestyle was rewarded with the knowledge that soon the time would come for his family to join him. Seven years of hard work and meticulous budgeting allowed him to pay passage for his wife child, parents, and siblings.

But still, he had loftier dreams. Life in the coal mines was tough. The Mandas traveled to Cleveland in 1921 and settled into a more comfortable life, as Louis made a career in the tool and die industry.

They were endlessly thankful for all they were given. They had each other, together as a family. Their new start in America, thanks to Louis' years of dedication to his dreams, gave them hope for the future. Life was good.

What is Financial Balance?

Financial balance is being a good steward of your resources, responsibly managing your cash flow and striving to eliminate all debt. Some of you may budget out your month on a piece of paper; others may prefer high-tech computer programs that spit out pie charts and graphs. Both ways can be seen as balanced because both ways develop mental habits to control and manage your wealth. However your preferred method, if your financial management is successfully working to responsibly control your cash flow and eliminate any debt, you are on the right track. We need money to survive. Financial balance gives us peace of mind. Financial wellness is closely linked to our sense of survival, stability, success, and significance.

Droughts are extremely stressful times for farmers because their fields are not yielding harvests. And these droughts affect us all in some small or big way. Like it or not, money can be the source of joy and the source of suffering. It nudges us at the very core of who we are, because we are so dependent on it. At the peak of the Great Depression, suicide rates went up from 12.1 to 18.9 people per 100,000.[19] This is just another example of how money can put the human person into crisis mode, cause us to lose focus of not only what our hopes and dreams are, but who we are altogether.

Living a Life of Significance: The Four S's

Most people live a life *by circumstance* instead of living a life *on purpose.* The following four basic categories sum up the stages most people live through or remain stuck in.

1. Survival

Working hard from paycheck to paycheck to make ends meet; working extra jobs, doing what you can to put food on the table and pay utilities; little or no savings account; always watching to see if checks clear, accumulating debts.

2. Stability

Able to meet monthly financial requirements. Have the ability to put small amounts into savings, take vacations, enjoy entertainment, managing debts.

3. Success

When you're able to live comfortably and save larger amounts of money, become debt free and accumulate some wealth, perhaps even have the ability to share your wealth with others. For example, taking family and friends on vacation; buying a family member a much-needed car or help them with other needs.

4. Significance

All your needs and desires are met and you begin to truly live for others. You create a legacy for your children and family, and make a difference in your community, church, and world. The phrase *first you must take care of yourself before you can take care of others* rings very true and can be implemented here. The airlines even tell you in the event of an emergency put on your oxygen mask first then assist others. Perhaps you have bought your freedom with financial success and can donate much time to causes dear to you with no expectation of monetary returns. Significance is a point in life when you no longer are bound by the ways of the world. Few people reach significance, however, I know that reaching any goal is first a decision then a discipline and a focused commitment to effort. You can reach significance if it's your heart's desire: your dream and goal to do so.

Why do I Need Financial Balance? (what's in it for me?)

Our dreams and goals are often wrapped up in our financial condition. If we see a bleak financial situation, we may translate that into a bleak future, with your dreams crushed and your hopes dashed. You may lose your sense of judgment and logic to find a solution to your financial woes. Or, simply put, you may be making a mountain out of a molehill. One thing is certain: panic over financial distress will not help you at all. If you have a leak in your boat, the quickest solution is to start bailing the water over the sides. In other words, immediate action is the quickest and most effective solution to financial distress.

EMOTIONAL & TRAUMA CAUSED BY FINANCIAL STRESS

Finances can paralyze you. Financial worries can cause you to wake up with night sweats. They can sow seeds of doubt and a loss of hope, cause fear of the future, and deter you from your dreams and goals. When your finances are out of alignment and you live in survival mode, losing a twenty dollar bill can cause you fret and worry. The loss of your entire wallet can cause sheer panic. Some people are losing hundreds of thousands of dollars on their retirement IRAs or 401Ks. Some are losing their homes and their cars, causing major stresses in all five areas of their lives.

BREAKDOWN IN RELATIONSHIPS

Any imbalance leads to dissention and quarrel because harmony between all five pillars has been lost. When I struggled with mathematics as a teenager, I remember being so angry that I would slam my books and stomp out of the room, trying hard not to slam the door on the way out. I would argue with my Dad, who was my math teacher at school and acted as my tutor at home, because I *just didn't get it!* This would cause tension in the entire household.

Money is said to be the number one topic of marital arguments. It seems ironic that the one thing that both husband and wife need, desire, and work for, gets in the way of marriages and family all the time. In today's world, husbands work harder than ever, more hours away from the family. Wives work even harder than their husbands, juggling both career work and the care of their family. Children are sent to daycare or latch-key; either way, they don't get the nurtured love of the parents as much as they should. And for what, to pay for the things they don't really need, or just to impress people they don't really care about, with the money they do not really have to spend! A wise friend has said to me, "Today's family farms out the wife to the highest bidder and the kids to the lowest bidder, with the husband being absent more than present at home. The result is stressful living and a 50% divorce rate, creating even more challenges." The emotional stress caused by poor financial alignment can get in the way of so many of your aspirations and break important, life-building relationships. When financial distress leads to marital stress, the domino effect has begun, and it is not so easy to stop the flow of imbalance and disaster.

"Money problems" is a simple way of vaguely defining a host of probable financial issues resulting in marital dissention:

- Unemployment

- Debt

- Ill-management

- Lack of money

- One spouse carries the load more than the other

- Wife not working and she resents it

- Wife not working and he resents it

- Wasteful spending and bad money habits: no sense of sacrifice

Dr. Dobson, Founder of *Focus on the Family*, shares a story of some courageous friends of his who chose to sacrifice excessive pleasures in pursuit of a life of balance:

Some friends of mind recently sold their house and moved into a smaller and less expensive place just so they could lower their payments and reduce the hours required in the workplace. That kind of downward mobility is almost unheard of today—it's almost un-American. But when we reach the end of our lives and we look back on the things that mattered most, those precious relationships with people we love will rank at the top of the list.

If friends and family will be a treasure to us then, why not live like we believe it today? That may be the best advice I have ever given anyone—and the most difficult to implement.

People today have not been taught how to practice delayed gratification. We need to learn to save bigger down payments before we make large purchases. CFO Don Tucker teaches entrepreneurs how to save more money for down payments with the following technique:

- First, ***establish the true need***. Or is it a "want"? Calculate the payment with your current down payment, and then discipline yourself to save the payment for an additional three to six months. At the end of the time frame, it should be clear to you whether this is a true need or if it was a temporary want.

- Second, as a bonus, you will have that much more saved money to put down, thus **reducing your total debt concern long-term**. Remember: it's tough to save money and earn interest when you're paying interest to debts.

How do I Apply Financial Balance?

SELF-KNOWLEDGE: TEMPERAMENT & LOVE LANGUAGE

Understanding your particular background can give you a clue to your attitudes towards money. For example, if you grew up in poverty, you may be inclined to hoard your possessions. Understanding your temperament is just as useful. Perhaps you are a very outgoing sanguine who loves to spend money on gifts for others and golfing weeks in Las Vegas with your friends. Perhaps you are an introverted phlegmatic who loses track of time in the evenings reading books and neglects to put time towards balancing your accounts.

What if your love language is Gifts, and you buy gifts for others to express your love for them and to make yourself feel good in the process. You put more importance on the gift-giving than on the person you are giving it to, because of the sheer enjoyment of giving. This behavior can lead you to spend much more money than is prudent, and can cause an accumulation of credit card debts. This is an example of how a love language can affect your finances. By becoming aware of your temperaments and love languages, you may come to a better understanding of your attitudes about money matters.

Mark's Thoughts:

When Linda and I got married, we didn't at first know it, but we had vastly different attitudes about money. She was raised with a mom who got the family paycheck, made purchases at will, and used credit as a way of life. I was raised to practice delayed gratification, save the money, do without at first so you can then pay cash. We paid cash in full for everything: vacations, cars, and clothes, the only exception being the house, on which we placed a 30% down payment.

I loved and trusted Linda, who naturally took over the stress of running the checkbook and household when we married. I thought it was awesome, until years later when we realized we had opposing views on money matters, and we were thousands of dollars in credit card debt. That was in addition to our mortgage debt. We were polar opposites when it came to money management decisions: I took a very Choleric approach and she took a laissez-faire approach. Eventually I took over the stress of money management and we began a journey to recovery. The first stop was a budget!

BUDGETING & DEBT

Looking back on my notes from when I first began meeting with Mark and began my journey as an E5 leader, I see that one of the first things we tackled was my financial welfare. I was almost embarrassed to talk to him about how I handled my finances, because I knew I was neglecting my responsibilities in this realm: I didn't know how much we were spending monthly, how much debt I had on my shoulders, and what our financial future looked like. I had an inkling that Meredith and I were living beyond our means (since our means were so meager) but didn't know to what extent. We had six different credit cards with balances on most. With help from Mark, my wife and I eliminated credit cards, created a debt-reduction plan by opening an alternate (savings) bank account, and even rediscovered a dormant account with $600 sitting there that I didn't even know about! We paid more than the monthly minimum on our credit cards, about $100 extra each month, in order to speed up the pay-off process, instead of eliminating the debt all at once. If we had paid it all off directly, we would not have had the necessary wiggle room to cover our basic needs. Even though we had to cover accumulated credit card interest, it was minimal. We were keeping ourselves from accumulating more credit card debt by covering our living expenses with my paycheck, not my card. By becoming more aware, using cash only, tithing properly, and practicing delayed gratification by not buying on a whim, we got a real grip and confidence on our financial situation. I remember Mark saying to me: "If you can't handle the little things, how will you be able to handle the bigger things to come?" This thought really provoked me to take hold of my financial situation and be more responsible. I went from a guy who simply spent and randomly wrote checks when necessary to a guy who reviewed every expenditure weekly and created a plan to reduce debt and increase savings. As a result, I felt more free and more confident.

Here is a Monthly Budgeting Plan that I have found very effective in its thoroughness and clarity:

Monthly Budget

Monthly Results (to fill at end of month)

Results:	M. Average	WK1	WK2	WK3	WK4	SAmount:
Total Income						
Necessary Expenses						
Discretionary Spending						
Total Spending						
Amount Remaining to Save or Use Wisely						

Monthly Income (to fill at end of month)

Income:	M. Average	WK1	WK2	WK3	WK4	SAmount:
· Primary Income						
Other Income						
Total Income						

Necessary Expenses

Payment:	M. Average	WK1	WK2	WK3	WK4	SAmount:
Mortgage						
Water						
House Gas						
Electric						
Car Insurance, Payments, Repairs						
Car Gas						
Student Loans P & M						
Food & Groceries						
Clothes						
Phone, Local						
Phone, Distance						
Healthcare						
Life Insurance						
House Insurance						
Home Repairs & Maintenance						
Child & Baby Expenses						
Other						
Charity / Tithing						
Total Necessary Expenses						

Discretionary Expenses

Payment:	M. Average	WK1	WK2	WK3	WK4	$Amount:
Credit Card Payment						
Internet / TV						
Landscape & Yard						
Entertainment						
Dining Out						
Travel & Vacation						
Computer Costs						
Recreation Center						
Total Discretionary Expenses						

Liabilities

Credit Card/Other:	Paid & Date	Interest Accruement @ %:	$Amount left / Date:
American Express			
Visa Key			
Kohls			
Student Loan #1			
Student Loan #2			
Car			
House			
Total Liability Expense			

HOME PURCHASING & TAXES

Home purchasing and taxes can be big sources of financial distress. There are many misconceptions about home purchasing etiquette that can lead to debt. The book *Taming the Money Monster* by Ron Blue is an excellent must-read on finances. He explains that most people who buy a house with little money down end up paying 1.5 to 3 times more than agreed to, because of interest accumulation. In many cases, after repairs, upkeep, and remodeling, along with taxes and insurance, you end up losing money, even after paying off the mortgage and selling it thirty years later. In other words, the theory of houses increasing in value over time is false.

Equally as false is the idea that there is a great tax advantage to owning a home. You pay more in the end and get less back. Let's talk squarely about taxes: Uncle Sam and local property tax collection will get their share, and no one can "beat the system." I'd rather have more cash in my pocket than larger debts, which are a result of my eagerness to buy before being properly financially equipped. If I didn't practice delayed gratification and save for a bigger down payment for my house, I could get myself into some seriously deep holes that take a lot of time and effort to escape.

Eliminating Unnecessary Spending

My wife and I had three major student loan amounts to pay off after we finished our education, and it was our goal to become debt free. We combed through our budget and spending habits and eliminated all impulse spending, and took on some side jobs to bring in a little extra cash flow. It was a period of frugality, but our positive attitudes and hopes for the future kept our days content. We felt fortunate without measure for all the blessings in our lives and believed that any extraneous spending was either a splurge for the good of the family, or if unplanned, a burden that kept us from our goals.

You may have to re-evaluate your spending habits in order to reach financial balance. Build new habits of checking your finances every week, eliminating wasteful spending, possibly downsizing your house or cars. The idea is *free living*: no debt. Not owned by anybody or anything. Increase cash flow so as to decrease debt.

There is always a corner that can be cut from our spending habits. This may seem like a given, that unnecessary spending can be eliminated. But let's take a moment and evaluate *what we consider necessary* and *what is truly necessary* (like food, shelter, and clothes).

Below is a chart of common money drainers. Fill out this chart to determine how you can trim your spending habits.

	Can I change my habits? (yes/no)	How?
Vacations (how often/how long)	*Yes*	*Stay 5 nights instead of 9 nights*
Vacations (how often/how long)		
Latest technology: phone, tv, computer, music		
Clothing		
Vehicle(s)		
Home Projects and Decorating		
Eating Out vs. Dining In		
Children's Activities: sports, dance, music, etc.		
Other insights I have		

How many people in your life do you know who take this attitude toward spending? Do you know someone who is 100% debt free? Do you know someone who takes on an attitude of responsible spending in order to achieve his or her dreams and goals? I would guarantee that at least 99% of us have goals in our 10-10-10 that require large sums of money to accomplish: a new home, travel, donation or goodwill.... With the right alignment in our lives and the appropriate cash flow management, you can be someone who makes a real difference in your life and the lives of others in your family, community, nation, and world.

With the right attitude toward spending, we experience freedom from things and freedom to attain other goals in life. We have all experienced the heavy burden that money can bring. *Freedom from financial burden is the key to financial balance, healthier lives, and better marriages.*

TITHING & GOODWILL

God blesses you with all that you have, including the things of this world. Because of this, we have the responsibility to give back to God: give to his Church and his people. We are not the only ones with an agenda; God has a Plan, too! He uses money as a tool to bring about his Goodness in the world.

If you give to God, he's going to give you more. His generosity can never be outdone. He is a God of plenty and promise.

1. **Tithing 10 Percent**

The Book of Deuteronomy tells us to tithe, "so that the Lord, your God, may bless you in all that you undertake" (Deut. 14:29). The tenth commandment, *You shall not covet your neighbors goods,* prohibits greed and the unlimited accumulation of goods. Tithing your money ensures that your attitude towards it is one of both detachment and trust. After all, you *do* get to keep 90% to spend or save how you like! My prayer for you is that you choose to use your money wisely so it can be a blessing to you, not a curse.

2. **Complete Trust**

Francis of Assisi was the son of a wealthy textile merchant. He had everything he needed and more: he wore the finest clothes in the richest colors, lived in an enviable home on the sloping hills of Assisi, and the liveliest of friends who would join him drinking and singing in the streets at all hours of the day and night.

He had a longing to live outside of his comfort zone and so decided to become a knight in the crusades to the East. This desire eventually led him to denounce all money and goods and become completely dependent on God's Providence. He lived his life in trust of God's generosity, with nothing but a common tunic, eating fish from the rivers and sleeping under the blanket of stars.

This was extreme trust at the expense of all worldly goods. God does not ask this of all of us, but even so, modern-day heroes such as Mother Teresa took the brave step to own little but her sari. The point we can take from these heroic examples is extreme trust. It takes an insurmountable measure of trust to tithe 10% when you are responsibly spending and still *just surviving*. It takes an insurmountable measure of trust when you see the mounting costs of college and have four children to provide for. It takes an insurmountable measure of trust when you work so hard for your paycheck, *just to see it passed on to someone else* (especially when you've lived your life buying stuff you don't really need while increasing your debt!). Build your trust through prayer: ask for it, simply. Trust in God and his unlimited generosity will not let you down.

Benefits of Financial Balance

When you are free from financial burden, this positively affects all other pillars of balance. Peace is able to take over all facets of your life, and you are able to concentrate on living your life to its fullest, without financial struggle or distraction.

However, it is important to keep in mind the bible passage: *From everyone who has been given much, much will be required* (Luke 12:48). Wealthy people still have to think about and manage their finances wisely. Ever hear of a lottery winner going broke shortly after the big win? This is more common than not, and takes place because the winner's culture of thought about money has not changed, even though their bank account has. Develop the proper thoughts about finances and you will achieve your dreams.

Furthermore, financial balance allows for the goals listed on your 10-10-10 that include financial backing to return from the "hopeless" to the "possible."

Be on top of it. Continue to equip yourself with personal finance capabilities so that you can not only maintain your wealth, eliminate your debt, but also build for your future.

Mark's Experience:

My personal story regarding finances could be a book unto itself! I shared a story earlier about my attitude regarding money versus my wife's attitude in our early marriage days. Early in my business career, after some mediocre successes, I invested poorly and spent too much money buying things I didn't need, all to impress people I didn't even know, and I almost went bankrupt. Not once... but twice! I repeated these mistakes without good mentorship in my life. I can therefore honestly say that I have lived in both sets of circumstances, and prefer to be free from the bondage money problems can bring.

My mentor taught me to know my finances at all times, to be prepared for the opportunity to make good decisions, and to invest my time for future growth. It would be a shame if I didn't prepare to win. He taught me techniques to get out of personal debt. He taught me how to strive to live a life free from financial bondage. I learned that through good stewardship I could gain another level of freedom. Part of good stewardship also meant I needed to start tithing properly (at least 10% of my income).

When you are debt free with no obligations and plenty of income, you have options. I decided I wanted those kinds of options. I got on a budget and we practiced delayed gratification and lived below our means. Through the process of E5, I learned to live with little and remain content. Within six years we became prosperous enough to buy luxury automobiles with cash. We paid off our credit card debts, we paid cash for our purchases, and we became free from financial bondage. What a tremendous load lifted off of me and my family! One of my dreams on my 10-10-10 early in the program of E5 was to pay for my children's college education in cash. We attained those dreams and goals. Our personal freedom became a blessing to others. When you have met the needs of your own family you can think about the needs of others.

It took me over a year with Mark to outline and organize my financial wellbeing. My wife and I were in debt up to our ears, paying off student loans and credit cards, and no savings to speak of. In a low-paying ministry position within the Church, and no budget plan in motion, there was no real hope of achieving debt-free living any time soon. Through the process of E5, I created a budget with Mark's help, listing all debts and their respective monthly payments. For the first time I had an idea of what kind of debt I was in and how long it would take to pay off. I knew, with a sanguine temperament, that I wasn't detail-oriented and inclined to make budget plans, but I knew I had to create habits to control what we spent and to create a plan to eliminate our debt. This required us to use cash more often than credit cards (we actually froze our credit cards in a block of ice in the freezer!), to track all expenditures, and to practice delayed gratification on a higher level than we had been. I knew how often I had to supplement my income painting houses, in order to live and to save. A few years into our budgeting system, we have increased our savings account by 6000%! This great victory had proven to us that we could reach our goal of being 100% debt free, including our house and our cars, and that we could be generous benefactors in our tithing and still come out ahead with the help of E5 principles leading the way.

E5 is about living in prosperity and abundance, not in desperation. Don't wait to get a grip on your finances, because the result of your determination is a greater peace of mind and a future of greater prosperity. Our utmost advice here: eliminate debt! Curb wasteful spending to achieve a status of debt-free living. *Debt-free living is the core of financial balance.*

PERSONAL ASSESSMENT: QUESTIONS & APPLICATIONS

Do I feel confident about my current financial situation? If so, why? If not, why not?

_____

_____

_____

_____

_____

Am I happy with the family's current monthly income amount? Why or why not?

_____

_____

_____

_____

_____

Am I a good steward of my resources? What makes me good or not good in this area?

_____

_____

_____

_____

_____

Have I submitted my financial reality over to God? If not, what keeps me from this?

_____

_____

_____

_____

_____

Am I living a life of Survival, Stability, Success, or Significance?

_____

_____

_____

_____

_____

CONCLUSION

Living a Life of Significance & Accomplishment

No eulogy is due to him who simply does his duty and nothing more.

~Augustine of Hippo

<u>You</u> can live a life of significance and accomplishment!

To be someone extraordinary takes extreme effort. This life is not for wimps: God is calling each of us to be extraordinary. To be this way, it takes extraordinary power. Just like a spaceship needs a ton of fuel to be blasted off to space, we need a ton of fuel to get us to where we belong: at the top. We have the capability of achieving. How do you want your life to play out? Would you like to be 80 years old, looking back at your life, with a sense of regret for the things you did not accomplish, or with a sense of accomplishment, knowing that you became the best possible person you could be, and achieved your dreams and goals in the process?

There is a method to anything of significance, and this book gives you the method to live your life without regrets, to dream big, to live without fear, and to achieve your dreams. This method is E5, living a life of equilibrium in all facets of your existence: spiritually, emotionally, mentally, physically and financially. A balanced life is a life that leads to peace, joy, and fulfillment. The natural by-product of balance, the 10-10-10, and Vertical Alignment, is **success**. Success and balance coincide; they are simultaneous in your journey.

Be self-aware. Your temperament, love language, and strengths are the blueprints of your identity. Help others become self-aware. Be generous and appreciative of those around you by your awareness of their temperaments and love languages. This is a pivotal aspect of communication and success.

Believe in yourself, because a lack of confidence can tear down the castle of dreams you have within your heart. Believe in your ability to be great, to accomplish great things, and to do it all alongside God, the One who has given you your dreams, and who believes in your ability to achieve them.

Life goes forward, with or without you. We get older regardless of our productivity, work ethic, relaxation time, or fitness. *Developing your own success is now in your hands.* This is your journey! Make your time left on planet earth count for yourself, your family, your fellow man, and be the best you that God intended you to be!

Your Plan of Action

- Develop a daily scripture reading habit. We recommend you start with the Gospels and continue through Acts and the Epistles.

- Write out vertical alignment and read it daily.

- Make your own 10-10-10 and read it daily.

- Find a trusted Mentor who can help you achieve your dreams and goals.

- Write out a few unique affirmations that are unique to your dreams and goals. Use the following two affirmations to get you started:

    a. Does this decision affect my life in a positive way over the next 2-5years? If not, don't do it.

    b. Does this decision move me closer to my dreams and goals or further away? If not, don't do it.

- Read the following list of books:

    » The Temperaments God Gave You by Art and Lorraine

Bennett. Take the assessment provided in the book.

» The 5 Love Languages by Gary Chapman. Take the assessment provided in the book.

» Now Discover your Strengths by Marcus Buckingham

» Talent is Never Enough by John Maxwell

- Become aware of the drivers and the hardwiring in you and use the knowledge to relate to others.

- Get a physical check-up and start paying attention to your overall wellbeing.

- Find a trusted advisor and create a financial analysis of your current position. Create a budget and stick with it with the goal in mind of eliminating your debts.

For additional resources, check out our website: www.e5leader.com

Contact us for personal coaching if you need additional help or if you would like us to speak to your group on the topic of E5 via the web.

GOD BLESS YOU!

> *What lies behind us and what lies before us are*
> *tiny matters compared to what lies within us.*
> *~Ralph Waldo Emerson*

LIST OF DEFINITIONS

Your "Cheat Sheet"
to Success

E5: A state of being in which you achieve equilibrium in all five areas (pillars) of life, which gives you the ability to pursue and achieve your life's dreams and goals.

Five Pillars: Five areas of life which are in need of balance (equilibrium): Spiritual, Emotional, Mental, Physical, Financial.

Balance: The achievement of equilibrium in all 5 pillars: Spiritual, Emotional, Mental, Physical, Financial (E5).

Vertical Alignment: The order and structure, to prioritize your thoughts, relationships, and time to aid you in your daily key decisions. Your checklist of true priorities includes, in order: God, Spouse (or parents), Children (or siblings), Family members/ Church/Community, Country, Job/School/Source of Income, Self.

10-10-10: A living and active list that contains your goals and dreams in three categories: *Monetary Self, Non-Monetary Self,* and *Others Monetary or Non-Monetary.* It is a critical visible reminder that you read over daily in order to align your daily thoughts and actions to a higher purpose.

Love Languages: Your primary and secondary communication codes for giving and receiving love. Namely: words of affirmation, acts of service, receiving gifts, quality time, physical touch.

Temperament: The God-given hard wiring of your behavior patterns. It is "one aspect of an individual's total personality – the aspect related to behavior and reaction."[20]

Choleric Temperament: A hard driver, ultimate Type A personality, decisive, a natural leader.

Sanguine Temperament: Loving, playful, life of the party.

Melancholic Temperament: Loves details and the order in which they belong.

Phlegmatic Temperament: Casually relaxed with just about everything, easy-going and peaceful at all costs.

Spiritual Life: The spiritual life is God's relationship with you, your relationship with God, and your continuous efforts to make this relationship more authentic and more genuine.

Spiritual Balance: The attainment of a God-centered life.

Emotional Balance: The ability to control your emotive thoughts and reactions to people, internal feelings, and external stimuli (input) with virtue, strength of character, and a clear objective at all times. Attainment of understanding the Who, What, How, and Why that makes up *you*.

Mental Balance: The ability to process all of life's demands in an orderly, balanced manner (mental toughness). Equips you to properly process and react to all demands and experiences in a way that will help you achieve your dreams and goals, without breaking any of man's laws or God's laws.

Physical Balance: Attainment of total physical harmony and wellness. The awareness of and application of healthy habits for your personal wellness which affects every other facet of life, including your personal relationships.

Financial Balance: Being a good steward of your resources, responsibly managing your cash flow and striving to eliminate all debt. Attainment of proper alignment of money through proper Culture of Thought.

Culture of Thought: The way we think due to environment and associations both past and present. We choose our own culture.

Positive Culture of Thought: A state of mind that is disciplined, joyful, kind, compassionate, moral, just, and willed with honor, integrity, and love. This state of mind is formed by good values, positive associations, and a helpful (not distracting) environment that will support you to achieve your dreams and goals.

Words of Affirmation: The words that give you the personal encouragement and confidence you need to achieve your goals and dreams. Words of life you sow into others.

Three Powers: Unique success principals that are invaluable habits that propel you to achieve your dreams and your goals.

Power of Submission: The choice to respect authority by releasing control for the betterment of self or others. Spiritually, it is the total union with God that includes *trust and loving, respectful obedience* to His Will;

Power of Unity: When two or more persons are in agreement and have formed a common bond which multiplies your capability to achieve. Spiritually, it is the power that comes from being united to God in his will, and united to others with whom you have meaningful relationships, especially within the living of Vertical Alignment.

Power of the Spoken Word: Brings your goals into existence through your words which give power.

The Four S's: The evolutions towards prosperity: Survival, Stability, Success, Significance. The use of E5 to pursue the Four S's is a process of prosperity in spiritual terms that connects us to God and others.

About the Authors

Mark Pierce was raised by his father in what he calls a "dysfunctional family," the third in line of four boys. As a teen, he was rambunctious, defiant, and couldn't wait to leave home. He went to a vocational school to study welding. Even though he was gifted in school, higher education was not part of his plans. At the age of 18, he graduated high school, worked as a welder, married his high school sweetheart, and welcomed his first child into the world. He quickly realized welding wasn't paying enough to support his family, and moved on to work in his father-in-law's tool and die shop. By the time he left the company after 6 years, Mark was the Sales Manager of a 12 million dollar territory for the tool and die company, learning all of his skill through experience, training, and mentorship.

After being told that he'd be a great entrepreneur, Mark began his own business that, in four years' time, he built to 12 million in revenues with a 20 million dollar order on the books for the following year. The appeal of the Good Life had Mark sell his business and take two years off to relax and play golf. He joined the Ben Hogan Mini Tour until he was running out of money and time. He realized that the needs of his growing family were paramount and so began another business. This second venture began what Mark calls his "downward spiral" which lasted ten years. When Norm Kizirian entered his life, Mark was thirsty for mentorship. Norm had the complete package: a good business, marriage, and spiritual life, and joy in his life. Norm put Mark on a path of discovery and learning unlike any other teaching he had experienced. He discovered books as tools for improvement. To date, Mark has attended 300 plus seminars, listened to over 3700 inspirational, motivational, educational CDs and read over 300 books on the topics of leadership and personal development.

After achieving stability in his second business, Mark invested time and energy in other ventures and found success again. He looked for mentorship with others every chance he got. One of his mentors recommended that he consider teaching others from his life's experiences on leadership and success, and thus began the journey as a business leadership coach. During his career, Mark has worked with over 3000 companies, driven a million miles, coached and mentored more than 130 individuals, and lived life with a passion.

Mark says of his accomplishments as a Business Leadership Coach and Mentor: "This book is a culmination of my life of mentoring and sowing seeds into others. Paul Koopman is one of those people who has made a difference in my life. He is an excellent student, a good friend, and a great husband and father. He has reflected these teachings into his life and now I am seeing my reflection through his success as he enters the world of leadership coaching."

Mark and Linda have been married for 33 happy years. They have four beautiful children together and reside in North Royalton, Ohio.

~

Paul Koopman spent his childhood in a happy home, the youngest of four children. He was always known as "Paully," the energetic clown, and appreciated for his quick wit and cheery disposition. He didn't display much interest in school and instead focused on sports, which developed into an obsession with golf in his high school years. His dream was to join the PGA Tour, and his extreme focus taught him discipline, commitment, and determination.

By age 18 Paul had met his future wife and was sure of his plans for the future: golf. But God had other plans! At the age of 20, the death of his father shook his world and began a journey of self-discovery that taught him invaluable lessons along the way. From working as a Shoe Truck Salesman to a Steel Packer to a Painter's Apprentice, Paul discovered that there was a part of him that had yet to be discovered, and he yearned to find his hidden talents and uncover his path to a life of meaningfulness. The decision to go back to school and get his undergraduate degree in history and theology gave him the opportunity to travel Europe which was a powerful stage of growth in his life. All within a period of one year, Paul married, graduated, welcomed his first child into the world, and began his career as a Youth Director.

During his second assignment as a Youth Director, and while he was finishing up his Master's Degree in Business, Paul met Mark. Thus began a long mentorship relationship and friendship that led to the discovery of his dreams and goals in life.

Paul's extensive experience in event coordination includes de-signing and directing numerous retreats, conferences, youth camps, and trips. He has also initiated, designed, and run men's groups with great success. He has spoken at numerous forums regarding faith and spiritual formation, and has acted as mentor to hundreds of teenagers throughout his years as Youth Director. Paul has extensive experience training, motivating, and directing dozens of adult volunteers within the church dynamic. His influ-ence as a leader to the young and old alike has produced concrete results of formation and balance in the lives of those he's touched. Paul has an extensive library on leadership, personal develop-ment, and spirituality, which has launched his passion to make a difference in the lives of others by helping them discover their capabilities, reach their fullest potential through E5, and achieve their dreams and goals.

Paul is currently President and Partner of YouCan, Inc., Partner of E5 Leader, LLC, and he continues to work in Youth Ministry. He is a John Maxwell Certified Coach and Trainer. Most importantly of all, Paul is a family man. The devotion he has for his wife and children has always been paramount in his life, and continues to be the driving force behind his personal betterment and success. He and Meredith currently reside in Strongsville, Ohio with their four beautiful children.

Notes

1   Bennett, Art & Larraine, *The Temperament God Gave You* (Manchester, New Hampshire: Sophia Institute Press, 2005), 6

2   Bennett, Art & Larraine, *The Temperament God Gave Your Spouse* (Manchester, New Hampshire: Sophia Institute Press, 2008), p. 61-2

3   Bennett, p. 77-9

4   Bennett, p.94-5

5   Bennett, p.109-10

6   Bennett, *The Temperament God Gave You*, 17-8.

7   Bennett, *The Temperament God Gave You, 18.*

8   Chapman, Gary, *The Five Love Languages: How to Express Heartfelt Commitment to Your Mate,* (Chicago: Northfield Publishing, 1995), p.186

9   Chapman p. 188

10   Chapman p. 190

11   Chapman p.192

12   Chapman p.194

13   Chapman, www.5lovelanguages.com /assessments/30-second-quizzes/love/

14   Bettger, Frank, 9.

15   Bettger, Frank, 12.

16   Bettger, Frank, *How I Raised Myself from Failure to Success in Selling* (New York, NY: Prentice Hall Press, 1986).

17   *Now, Discover Your Strengths*

18   Buckingham and Clifton, *Now, Discover your Strengths* (New York: The Free Press, 2001), p. 81-116. The list of strengths and definitions of strengths have been pulled from Chapter 4.

19   *Historical Statistics of the United States: Bicentennial Edition, Colonial Times to 1970*, Vol. 1 (Washington DC: 1975), 58, http://www2.census.gov/prod2/statcomp/documents/CT1970p1-03.pdf, accessed 2 February 2009.

20   Bennett, Art & Larraine, *The Temperament God Gave You*, 6. Ron Blue Taming the Money monster p.114 Strength Finders p. 96